WHITE COLLAR CRIME- SUPREME COURT'S LEADING CASE LAWS

CASE NOTES- FACTS- FINDINGS OF APEX COURT
JUDGES & CITATIONS

JAYPRAKASH BANSILAL SOMANI

Made with ♥ on the Notion Press Platform
www.notionpress.com

All the Past & Present Judges of the Supreme Court of India.

Salute to their wisdom.

Salute to their interpretation of Law.

Salute to their elaborative judgement writing.

Contents

Contents

Preface

Dear Learned Advocates of the Special Courts, Trial Courts, Session Courts, High Courts, Supreme Court & Individuals, Leaders, Officers,

I am very delighted to provide you a book on 'WHITE COLLAR CRIME'-Supreme Court of India Leading Case Laws.

In this book you will get...

1. Name of the Case i. e. Cause title

2.Relevant Sections discussed in the case

3. Hon'ble Judges/Coram of the case

4.Number of PDF Pages in Original Judgement of the case

5. All available Citations of the case

6. Case Note with appeal allowed/ dismissed or disposed off

7. Facts of the case

8. Hon'ble Apex Court's findings, while dismissing/allowing or disposing the appeal

9. Ratio Decidendi if any.

My special thanks to Manupatra, because of their web portal I can compile this book in well manner. I am also thankful to Notion Press to support me to publish & market this book throughout the Country. Thanks to my Juniors, Advocate Colleagues & Insolvency Professional Colleagues to support me in this venture.

Miss Shruti Kriti has helped me a lot to compile this book.

I hope this book will add some value addition in the wealth of your legal knowledge. Your positive feedbacks will boost me to compile/ write further books & negative feedbacks will improve my skills. Kindly send your valuable feedbacks by email.

Thanks with Regards,

Jayprakash B. Somani

Advocate, Supreme Court of India

Email: jaysomani64@gmail.com

Web Site:www.jayprakashsomani.com

Call: 9322188701, 8459194576

Acknowledgements

Printed & Published by
Notion Press
No. 8, 3rd Cross Street,
CIT Colony, Mylapore,
Chennai, Tamil Nadu- 600004

Managed by
Jayprakash Somani Advocates & Solicitors
Law Firm for Supreme Court of India
Delhi Office
B- 851, 1st Floor, Shivaji Marg, New Ashok Nagar, Delhi 110096.
Call: 9322188701, 8459194576

Supreme Court Chamber
312, 3rd Floor, M. C. Setalvad Block, In front of 'D' Gate, Bhagwan Das Road, Supreme Court of India, New Delhi 110001
Contact: 8459194576, 9811011747
www.jayprakashsomani.com

Books are available online in India

1. **Notion Press:**https://notionpress.com/author/jayprakash_somani
2. **Amazon:**https://www.amazon.in/s?k=jayprakash+somani
3. **Flipkart:**https://www.flipkart.com/search?q=Jayprakash%20Somani

Books are available online at International Market

4. **Amazon International:** https://www.amazon.com/s?k=jayprakash+somani
5. **Amazon United Kingdom:** https://www.amazon.co.uk/s?k=jayprakash+somani
6. **E-Books/Kindle edition at National & International Level:** https://www.amazon.in/s?k=jaypraksh+somani

CHAPTER ONE

Mallada K. Sri Ram Vs. The State of Telangana and Ors., 2022

Hon'ble Judges/Coram: Dr. D.Y. Chandrachud and Surya Kant, JJ.

Act/ Sections: Constitution of India - Article 22, Constitution of India - Article 226; Defence of India Act; Defence of India Rules - Rule 30, Defence of India Rules - Rule 30(1); Indian Penal Code, 1860 (IPC) - Section 120B, Indian Penal Code, 1860 (IPC) - Section 406, Indian Penal Code, 1860 (IPC) - Section 407, Indian Penal Code, 1860 (IPC) - Section 408, Indian Penal Code, 1860 (IPC) - Section 409, Indian Penal Code, 1860 (IPC) - Section 417, Indian Penal Code, 1860 (IPC) - Section 418, Indian Penal Code, 1860 (IPC) - Section 419, Indian Penal Code, 1860 (IPC) - Section 420, Indian Penal Code, 1860 (IPC) - Section 506; Telangana Prevention Of Dangerous Activities Of Boot-leggers, Dacoits, Drug-offenders, Goondas, Immoral Traffic Offenders Land-grabbers, Spurious Seed Offenders, Insecticide Offenders, Fertiliser Offenders, Food Adulteration Offenders, Fake Document Offenders, Scheduled Commodities Offenders, Forest Offenders, Gaming Offenders, Sexual Offenders, Explosive Substances Offenders, Arms Offenders, Cyber Crime Offenders And White Collar Or Financial Offenders Act, 1986 - Section 2(a), Telangana Prevention Of Dangerous Activities Of Boot-leggers, Dacoits, Drug-offenders, Goondas, Immoral Traffic Offenders Land-grabbers, Spurious Seed Offenders, Insecticide Offenders, Fertiliser Offenders, Food Adulteration Offenders, Fake Document Offenders, Scheduled Commodities Offenders, Forest Offenders, Gaming Offenders, Sexual Offenders, Explosive Substances Offenders, Arms Offenders, Cyber Crime Offenders And White Collar Or

Financial Offenders Act, 1986 - Section 2(x), Telangana Prevention Of Dangerous Activities Of Boot-leggers, Dacoits, Drug-offenders, Goondas, Immoral Traffic Offenders Land-grabbers, Spurious Seed Offenders, Insecticide Offenders, Fertiliser Offenders, Food Adulteration Offenders, Fake Document Offenders, Scheduled Commodities Offenders, Forest Offenders, Gaming Offenders, Sexual Offenders, Explosive Substances Offenders, Arms Offenders, Cyber Crime Offenders And White Collar Or Financial Offenders Act, 1986 - Section 3(2), Telangana Prevention Of Dangerous Activities Of Boot-leggers, Dacoits, Drug-offenders, Goondas, Immoral Traffic Offenders Land-grabbers, Spurious Seed Offenders, Insecticide Offenders, Fertiliser Offenders, Food Adulteration Offenders, Fake Document Offenders, Scheduled Commodities Offenders, Forest Offenders, Gaming Offenders, Sexual Offenders, Explosive Substances Offenders, Arms Offenders, Cyber Crime Offenders And White Collar Or Financial Offenders Act, 1986 - Section 12; Telangana Protection of Depositors of Financial Establishment Act, 1999

No. of pages of the Original Judgement: 09

Citation: MANU/SC/0444/2022

Case Note: Criminal - Order of detention - Challenge thereto - Section 2(x) of the Telangana Act of 1986 - Division Bench of the High Court dismissed the petition challenging detention order, hence present appeal - Whether order of detention which has been passed against the detenu is liable to be quashed?

Facts: An order of detention was passed against the detenu under the provisions of Section 3(2) of the Telangana Prevention of Dangerous Activities of Bootleggers, Dacoits, Drug-Offenders, Goondas, Immoral Traffic Offenders, Land Grabbers, Spurious Seed Offenders, Insecticide Offenders, Fertiliser Offenders, Food Adulteration Offenders, Fake Document Offenders, Scheduled Commodities Offenders, Forest Offenders, Gaming Offenders, Sexual Offenders, Explosive Substances Offenders, Arms Offenders, Cyber Crime Offenders and White Collar or Financial Offenders Act 1986. The order of detention was challenged before the High Court in a petition under Article 226 of the Constitution. The Division Bench of the High Court dismissed the petition by its impugned judgment and order. The Appellant, submits that there is ex facie, non-application of mind by the detaining authority while passing the order of detention. It was further submitted that it is evident from the recording of facts that the order of detention was passed nearly seven and five months after both the criminal cases were instituted. The detention was, based on stale material.

Hon'ble Apex Court Held, while allowing the appeal: 1. The order of detention notes that that the detenu is a 'white-collar offender' under Section 2(x) of the Telangana Act of 1986 whose offence of cheating gullible job aspirants has been causing "large scale fear and panic among the gullible unemployed job aspirants/youth and thus he has been acting in a manner prejudicial to the maintenance of public order apart from disturbing the peace, tranquility and social harmony in the society". These alleged offences were noted as the grounds for his detention, in addition to the apprehension that "he may violate the bail conditions and there is an imminent possibility of his committing similar offences, which would be detrimental to public order, unless he is prevented from doing so by an appropriate order of detention".

2. At this stage, it would also be material to note that the first case was registered on 15 October 2020, while the second case was registered on 17 December 2020. Bail was granted on 8 January 2021. The order of detention was passed on 19 May 2021 and was executed on 26 June 2021. The order of detention was passed nearly seven months after the registration of the first FIR and about five months after the registration of the second FIR. The order of detention is evidently based on stale material and demonstrates non-application of mind on the part of the detaining authority to the fact that the conditions which were imposed on the detenu, while granting bail, were duly fulfilled and there was no incidence of a further violation. In the counter affidavit which was filed before the High Court, the detaining authority expressed only an apprehension that the acts on the basis of which the FIRs were registered were likely to be repeated in the future, thereby giving rise to an apprehension of a breach of public order. The High Court has failed to probe the existence of a live and proximate link between the past cases and the need to detain the detenu after seven months of registration of the first FIR and nearly five months of securing bail.

3. A mere apprehension of a breach of law and order is not sufficient to meet the standard of adversely affecting the "maintenance of public order". In this case, the apprehension of a disturbance to public order owing to a crime that was reported over seven months prior to the detention order has no basis in fact. The apprehension of an adverse impact to public order is a mere surmise of the detaining authority, especially when there have been no reports of unrest since the detenu was released on bail on 8 January 2021

and detained with effect from 26 June 2021. The nature of the allegations against the detenu are grave. However, the personal liberty of an Accused cannot be sacrificed on the altar of preventive detention merely because a person is implicated in a criminal proceeding. The powers of preventive detention are exceptional and even draconian. Tracing their origin to the colonial era, they have been continued with strict constitutional safeguards against abuse. Article 22 of the Constitution was specifically inserted and extensively debated in the Constituent Assembly to ensure that the exceptional powers of preventive detention do not devolve into a draconian and arbitrary exercise of state authority. The case at hand is a clear example of non-application of mind to material circumstances having a bearing on the subjective satisfaction of the detaining authority. The two FIRs which were registered against the detenu are capable of being dealt by the ordinary course of criminal law.

4. The impugned judgment of the High Court is set aside. The order of detention which has been passed against the detenu shall accordingly stand quashed and set aside. Appeal allowed.

CHAPTER TWO

Banka Sneha Sheela Vs. The State of Telangana and Ors., 2021

Hon'ble Judges/Coram: Rohinton Fali Nariman and Hrishikesh Roy, JJ.

Act/ Sections: Andhra Pradesh Prohibition Act, 1995; Bihar Control of Crimes Act, 1981; Code of Criminal Procedure, 1973 (CrPC) - Section 144; Constitution of India - Article 19, Constitution of India - Article 19(2), Constitution of India - Article 19(3), Constitution of India - Article 19(4), Constitution of India - Article 21, Constitution of India - Article 22, Constitution of India - Article 22(1), Constitution of India - Article 22(2), Constitution of India - Article 22(3), Constitution of India - Article 22(5); Defence of India Act - Section 3, Defence of India Act - Section 3(15); Defence of India Rules - Rule 30, Defence of India Rules - Rule 30(1); Drugs and Cosmetics Act, 1940; Indian Penal Code, 1860 (IPC) - Section 406, Indian Penal Code, 1860 (IPC) - Section 407, Indian Penal Code, 1860 (IPC) - Section 408, Indian Penal Code, 1860 (IPC) - Section 409, Indian Penal Code, 1860 (IPC) - Section 417, Indian Penal Code, 1860 (IPC) - Section 418, Indian Penal Code, 1860 (IPC) - Section 419, Indian Penal Code, 1860 (IPC) - Section 420, Indian Penal Code, 1860 (IPC) - Section 506; Telangana Prevention Of Dangerous Activities Of Boot-leggers, Dacoits, Drug-offenders, Goondas, Immoral Traffic Offenders Land-grabbers, Spurious Seed Offenders, Insecticide Offenders, Fertiliser Offenders, Food Adulteration Offenders, Fake Document Offenders, Scheduled Commodities Offenders, Forest Offenders, Gaming Offenders, Sexual Offenders, Explosive Substances Offenders, Arms Offenders, Cyber Crime Offenders And White Collar Or Financial Offenders Act, 1986 - Section

2(a), Telangana Prevention Of Dangerous Activities Of Boot-leggers, Dacoits, Drug-offenders, Goondas, Immoral Traffic Offenders Land-grabbers, Spurious Seed Offenders, Insecticide Offenders, Fertiliser Offenders, Food Adulteration Offenders, Fake Document Offenders, Scheduled Commodities Offenders, Forest Offenders, Gaming Offenders, Sexual Offenders, Explosive Substances Offenders, Arms Offenders, Cyber Crime Offenders And White Collar Or Financial Offenders Act, 1986 - Section 2(x), Telangana Prevention Of Dangerous Activities Of Boot-leggers, Dacoits, Drug-offenders, Goondas, Immoral Traffic Offenders Land-grabbers, Spurious Seed Offenders, Insecticide Offenders, Fertiliser Offenders, Food Adulteration Offenders, Fake Document Offenders, Scheduled Commodities Offenders, Forest Offenders, Gaming Offenders, Sexual Offenders, Explosive Substances Offenders, Arms Offenders, Cyber Crime Offenders And White Collar Or Financial Offenders Act, 1986 - Section 3

No. of pages of the Original Judgement: 15

Citation: AIR2021SC3656, (2021)9SCC415, MANU/SC/0493/2021

Case Note: Criminal - Preventive Detention - Complaints of fraud and cheating - Challenge against order directing detention dismissed - Section 3(2) of the Telangana Prevention of Dangerous Activities of Bootleggers, Dacoits, Drug-Offenders, Goondas, Immoral Traffic Offenders Land-Grabbers, Spurious Seed Offenders, Insecticide Offenders, Fertiliser Offenders, Food Adulteration Offenders, Fake Document Offenders, Scheduled Commodities Offenders, Forest Offenders, Gaming Offenders, Sexual Offenders, Explosive Substances Offenders, Arms Offenders, Cyber Crime Offenders and White Collar or Financial Offenders Act, 1986 (Act) - Whether dismissal of petition challenging detention order justified?

Facts: The present appeal was filed against the order dismissing Petitioner's writ petition filed to challenge Preventive Detention Order passed against her husband. The detention order referred five FIRs filed against the Detenu under Sections 420, 406 and 506 of the Indian Penal Code, 1860. Acts alleged caused loss of faith and trust among investors in stock trading fearing similar cheating. The activities alleged to also cause to be disturbance in the public.

Hon'ble Apex Court Held, while allowing the Appeals: For 'public order' to be disturbed, there must in turn be public disorder. Mere contravention of law such as indulging in cheating or criminal breach of trust certainly affects 'law and order' but before it can be said to affect 'public order', it must affect the community or the public at large.

There can be no doubt that what is alleged in the five FIRs pertain to the realm of 'law and order' in that various acts of cheating are ascribed to the Detenu which are punishable under the three Sections of the Indian Penal Code set out in the five FIRs. A close reading of the Detention Order would make it clear that the reason for the said Order is not any apprehension of widespread public harm, danger or alarm but is only because the Detenu was successful in obtaining anticipatory bail/bail from the Courts in each of the five FIRs. If a person is granted anticipatory bail/bail wrongly, there are well-known remedies in the ordinary law to take care of the situation. The State can always appeal against the bail order granted and/or apply for cancellation of bail. The mere successful obtaining of anticipatory bail/ bail orders being the real ground for detaining the Detenu, there can be no doubt that the harm, danger or alarm or feeling of security among the general public spoken of in Section 2(a) of the Telangana Prevention of Dangerous Activities Act is make believe and totally absent in the facts of the present case.

On the facts of this case, a possible apprehension of breach of law and order can be said to be made out if it is apprehended that the Detenu, if set free, will continue to cheat gullible persons. This may be a good ground to appeal against the bail orders granted and/or to cancel bail but certainly cannot provide the springboard to move under a preventive detention statute. Detention order quashed on this ground. The impugned judgment is set aside and the Detenu is ordered to be freed forthwith. Accordingly, the appeal is allowed.

CHAPTER THREE

P. Chidambaram Vs. Directorate of Enforcement, 2019

Hon'ble Judges/Coram: R. Banumathi and A.S. Bopanna, JJ.

Act/ Sections: Code of Criminal Procedure, 1973 (CrPC) - Section 438, Code of Criminal Procedure, 1973 (CrPC) - Section 482, Code of Criminal Procedure, 1973 (CrPC) - Section 491; Constitution of India - Article 14, Constitution of India - Article 20, Constitution of India - Article 20(1), Constitution of India - Article 20(3), Constitution of India - Article 21; Evidence Act - Section 145, Evidence Act - Section 161; Explosives Substances Act, 1908; Indian Penal Code, 1860 (IPC) - Section 26, Indian Penal Code, 1860 (IPC) - Section 120B, Indian Penal Code, 1860 (IPC) - Section 420; Narcotic Drugs and Psychotropic Substances Act, 1985; Prevention of Corruption (Amendment) Act, 2008; Prevention of Corruption (Amendment) Act, 2009; Prevention of Corruption (Amendment) Act, 2013; Prevention of Corruption (Amendment) Act, 2018; Prevention Of Corruption Act, 1988 - Section 8, Prevention Of Corruption Act, 1988 - Section 13, Prevention Of Corruption Act, 1988 - Section 13(1), Prevention Of Corruption Act, 1988 - Section 13(2); Prevention Of Money-laundering (forms And The Manner Of Forwarding A Copy Of Order Of Arrest Of A Person Along With The Material To The Adjudicating Authority And Its Period Of Retention) Rules, 2005 - Rule 3; Prevention of Money-Laundering (Forms, Search and Seizure or Freezing and the Manner of Forwarding the Reasons and Material to the Adjudicating Authority, Impounding and Custody of Records and the period of Retention) Rules, 2005; Prevention Of Money-laundering (manner Of

Forwarding A Copy Of The Order Of Provisional Attachment Of Property Along With The Material, And Copy Of Material In Respect Of Survey, To The Adjudicating Authority And Its Period Of Retention) Rules, 2005 - Rule 3; Prevention Of Money-laundering Act, 2002 - Section 2(1), Prevention Of Money-laundering Act, 2002 - Section 3, Prevention Of Money-laundering Act, 2002 - Section 4, Prevention Of Money-laundering Act, 2002 - Section 5, Prevention Of Money-laundering Act, 2002 - Section 5(2), Prevention Of Money-laundering Act, 2002 - Section 17, Prevention Of Money-laundering Act, 2002 - Section 19, Prevention Of Money-laundering Act, 2002 - Section 19(1), Prevention Of Money-laundering Act, 2002 - Section 19(3), Prevention Of Money-laundering Act, 2002 - Section 45, Prevention Of Money-laundering Act, 2002 - Section 45(1), Prevention Of Money-laundering Act, 2002 - Section 55, Prevention Of Money-laundering Act, 2002 - Section 56, Prevention Of Money-laundering Act, 2002 - Section 57, Prevention Of Money-laundering Act, 2002 - Section 58, Prevention Of Money-laundering Act, 2002 - Section 59, Prevention Of Money-laundering Act, 2002 - Section 60, Prevention Of Money-laundering Act, 2002 - Section 61, Prevention Of Money-laundering Act, 2002 - Section 65, Prevention Of Money-laundering Act, 2002 - Section 71, Prevention Of Money-laundering Act, 2002 - Section 73

No. of pages of the Original Judgement:24

Citation: AIR2019SC4198, (2019)9SCC24, MANU/SC/1209/2019

Case Note: Criminal - Anticipatory bail - Denial of - Sections 120B and 420 of Code of Criminal Procedure, 1973, Section 8 and Section 13(2) read with Section 13(1)(d) of Prevention of Corruption Act, 1988 and Sections 3 and 4 of Prevention of Money-Laundering Act, 2002 - CBI registered FIR under Section 120B of Code read with Section 420 of Code, Section 8 and Section 13(2) read with Section 13(1)(d) of Act against Accused for alleged irregularities in Foreign Investment Promotion Board (FIPB) clearance given to company for receiving foreign investment - Enforcement Directorate also registered case against accused persons for allegedly committing offence punishable under Sections 3 and 4 of Act - Appellant moved High Court seeking anticipatory bail in both cases - High Court rejected Appellant's plea for anticipatory bail in both cases - Hence, present appeal - Whether Appellant entitled for anticipatory bail.

Facts: CBI registered FIR under Section 120B Indian Penal Code read with Section 420 Indian Penal Code, Section 8 and Section 13(2) read with Section 13(1)(d) of the Prevention of Corruption Act, 1988 against the

Accused for the alleged irregularities in giving FIPB's clearance to company to receive overseas funds. On the basis of the said FIR registered by CBI, the Enforcement Directorate registered a case against the Accused persons for allegedly committing the offence punishable under Sections 3 and 4 of Act. The Appellant moved High Court seeking anticipatory bail in both cases. The High Court dismissed the application refusing to grant anticipatory bail to the Appellant by holding that it was a classic case of money-laundering. The Single Judge dismissed the application for anticipatory bail by holding that the alleged irregularities committed by the Appellant makes out a prima facie case for refusing pre-arrest bail to the Appellant.

Hon'ble Apex Court Held, while dismissing the appeal: (i) In terms of Section 4 of the PMLA, the offence of money-laundering was punishable with rigorous imprisonment for a term not less than three years extending to seven years and with fine. The Second Schedule to the Code of Criminal Procedure relates to classification of offences against other laws and in terms of the Second Schedule of the Code, an offence which is punishable with imprisonment for three years and upward but not more than seven years is a cognizable and non-bailable offence. Thus, Section 4 of the Act read with the Second Schedule of the Code makes it clear that the offences under the PMLA are cognizable offences. Section 420 of Indian Penal Code, Section 8 of the Prevention of Corruption Act was then found a mention in Part A of the Schedule. Section 420 Indian Penal Code, Section 8 of the Prevention of Corruption Act is punishable for a term extending to seven years. Thus, the essential requirement of Section 45 of PMLA Accused of an offence punishable for a term of imprisonment of more than three years under Part A of the Schedule was satisfied making the offence under PMLA. There was no merit in the contention of the Appellant that very registration of the FIR against the Appellant under PMLA was not maintainable.

(ii) As rightly submitted by Respondent that if the Accused were to be confronted with the materials which were collected by the prosecution/ Enforcement Directorate with huge efforts, it would lead to devastating consequences and would defeat the very purpose of the investigation into crimes, in particular, white collar offences. If the contention of the Appellant was to be accepted, the investigating agency would have to question each and every Accused such materials collected during investigation and in this process, the investigating agency would be exposing the evidence collected by them with huge efforts using their men and resources and this would give a chance to the Accused to tamper with the evidence and to destroy the money trail apart from paving the way for the Accused to influence the witnesses. If the contention of the Appellant was to be accepted that the Accused would have to be questioned with the materials and the investigating agency has to satisfy the court that the Accused was evasive during interrogation, the court would have to undertake a mini trial of scrutinizing the matter at intermediary stages of investigation like interrogation of the Accused and the answers elicited from the Accused and to find out whether the answers given by the Accused are evasive or whether they were satisfactory or not. This could have never been the intention of the legislature either under PMLA or any other statute.

(iii) Grant of anticipatory bail at the stage of investigation may frustrate the investigating agency in interrogating the Accused and in collecting the useful information and also the materials which might have been concealed. Success in such interrogation would elude if the Accused knows that he is protected by the order of the court. Grant of anticipatory bail, particularly in economic offences would definitely hamper the effective investigation. Having regard to the materials said to have been collected by the Respondent-Enforcement Directorate and considering the stage of the investigation, this court was of the view that it was not a fit case to grant anticipatory bail.

(iv) In a case of money-laundering where it involves many stages of placement, layering i.e. funds moved to other institutions to conceal origin and interrogation i.e. funds used to acquire various assets, it requires systematic and analysed investigation which would be of great advantage. As held in case of Anil Sharma, success in such interrogation would elude if the Accused knows that he is protected by a pre-arrest bail order. Section 438 Code of Criminal Procedure is to be invoked only in exceptional cases where the case alleged is frivolous or groundless. In the case in hand, there were allegations of laundering the proceeds of the crime. The Enforcement Directorate claims to have certain specific inputs from various sources, including overseas banks. Letter rogatory was also said to have been issued and some response have been received by the department. Having regard to the nature of allegations and the stage of the investigation, the investigating agency had to be given sufficient freedom in the process of investigation. Though this court did not endorse the approach of the Single Judge in extracting the note produced by the Enforcement Directorate, there was no ground warranting interference with the impugned order. Considering the facts and circumstances of the case, grant of anticipatory bail to the

Appellant would hamper the investigation and this was not a fit case for exercise of discretion to grant anticipatory bail to the Appellant.

Ratio Decidendi: Grant of anticipatory bail, particularly in economic offences would definitely hamper the effective investigation.

CHAPTER FOUR

Rohit Tandon Vs. The Enforcement Directorate, 2017

Hon'ble Judges/Coram: Dipak Misra, C.J.I., A.M. Khanwilkar and D.Y. Chandrachud, JJ.

Act/ Sections: Prevention of Money-Laundering Act, 2002 - Section 2(1), Prevention of Money-Laundering Act, 2002 - Section 3, Prevention of Money-Laundering Act, 2002 - Section 4, Prevention of Money-Laundering Act, 2002 - Section 19, Prevention of Money-Laundering Act, 2002 - Section 24, Prevention of Money-Laundering Act, 2002 - Section 44, Prevention of Money-Laundering Act, 2002 - Section 45, Prevention of Money-Laundering Act, 2002 - Section 45A, Prevention of Money-Laundering Act, 2002 - Section 45(1), Prevention of Money-Laundering Act, 2002 - Section 50, Prevention of Money-Laundering Act, 2002 - Section 50(4), Prevention of Money-Laundering Act, 2002 - Section 65, Prevention of Money-Laundering Act, 2002 - Section 71; Prevention of Corruption Act, 1988 - Section 12; Prevention of Money-Laundering (Amendment) Act, 2012 [Repealed];Prevention of Money-Laundering (Amendment) Act, 2005;Code of Criminal Procedure, 1973 (CrPC) - Section 5, Code of Criminal Procedure, 1973 (CrPC) - Section 155, Code of Criminal Procedure, 1973 (CrPC) - Section 172, Code of Criminal Procedure, 1973 (CrPC) - Section 177(1), Code of Criminal Procedure, 1973 (CrPC) - Section 439; Maharashtra Control of Organised Crime Act, 1999 - Section 21(4); Indian Penal Code, 1860 (IPC) - Section 34, Indian Penal Code, 1860 (IPC) - Section 109, Indian Penal Code, 1860 (IPC) - Section 120B, Indian Penal Code, 1860 (IPC) - Section 188, Indian Penal Code, 1860 (IPC) -

Section 406, Indian Penal Code, 1860 (IPC) - Section 409, Indian Penal Code, 1860 (IPC) - Section 420, Indian Penal Code, 1860 (IPC) - Section 467, Indian Penal Code, 1860 (IPC) - Section 468, Indian Penal Code, 1860 (IPC) - Section 471; Constitution of India - Article 14, Constitution of India - Article 21, Constitution of India - Article 32

No. of pages of the Original Judgement: 17

Citation: AIR2017SC5309, (2018)11SCC46, MANU/SC/1403/2017

Case Note: Criminal - Rejection of bail - Challenged thereto - Sections 3, 4 and 45 of Prevention of Money Laundering Act, 2002 - Appellant was arrested in connection with criminal case registered under Sections 3 and 4 of Act - Appellant first approached Additional Sessions Judge for releasing him on bail by way of application - Bail application came to be rejected - Appellant thereafter approached High Court by way of bail application and interlocutory application filed therein - High Court rejected prayer for bail vide impugned judgment - Hence, present appeal - Whether Appellant was entitled for enlargement on bail

Facts: The Appellant was arrested in connection with criminal case registered under Sections 3 and 4 of the Prevention of Money-Laundering Act, 2002. The Appellant first approached the Additional Sessions Judge for releasing him on bail by way of an application. The said bail application came to be rejected vide judgment by the said Court. The Appellant thereafter approached the High Court by way of bail application and an interlocutory application filed therein. The High Court independently considered the merits of the arguments but eventually rejected the prayer for bail vide impugned judgment. Hence, present appeal.

Hon'ble Apex Court Held, while dismissing the appeal: (i) The Appellant has not succeeded in persuading us about the inapplicability of the threshold stipulation under Section 45 of the Act. Present Court also noted the inexplicable silence or reluctance of the Appellant in disclosing the source from where such huge value of demonetized currency and also new currency has been acquired by him. The prosecution was relying on statements of many witnesses/accused already recorded, out of which few were considered by High Court. The same makes out a formidable case about the involvement of the Appellant in commission of a serious offence of money-laundering. It was, therefore, not possible for to record satisfaction that there were reasonable grounds for believing that the Appellant was not guilty of such offence. Further, the Lower Courts have justly adverted to the antecedents of the Appellant for considering the prayer for bail and concluded that it was not possible to hold that the Appellant was not likely to commit any offence ascribable to the Act of 2002 while on bail. Since the threshold stipulation predicated in Section 45 has not been overcome, the question of considering the efficacy of other points urged by the Appellant to persuade the Court to favour the Appellant with the relief of regular bail would be of no avail.

(ii) The fact that no limit for deposit was specified, would not extricate the Appellant from explaining the source from where such huge amount has been acquired, possessed or used by him. The volume of demonetized currency recovered from the office and residential premises of the Appellant, including the bank drafts in favour of fictitious persons and also the new currency notes for huge amount, leave no manner of doubt that it was the outcome of some process or activity connected with the proceeds of crime projecting the property as untainted property. No explanation has been offered by the Appellant to dispel the legal presumption of the property being proceeds of crime. Similarly, the fact that the Appellant has made declaration in the Income Tax Returns and paid tax as per law does not extricate the Appellant from disclosing the source of its receipt. No provision in the taxation laws has been brought to notice which grants immunity to the Appellant from prosecution for an offence of money-laundering. In other words, the property derived or obtained by the Appellant was the result of criminal activity relating to a scheduled offence. The argument of the Appellant that there was no allegation in the charge-sheet filed in the scheduled offence case or in the prosecution complaint that the unaccounted cash deposited by the Appellant was the result of criminal activity, would not come to the aid of the Appellant. That would have to be negatived in light of the materials already on record. The possession of such huge quantum of demonetized currency and new currency, without disclosing the source from where it was received and the purpose for which it was received, the Appellant had failed to dispel the legal presumption that he was involved in money-laundering and the property was proceeds of crime.

CHAPTER FIVE

Khaja Bilal Ahmed Vs. State of Telangana and Ors., 2019

Hon'ble Judges/Coram: Dr. D.Y. Chandrachud and Hrishikesh Roy, JJ.

Act/ Sections: Cyber Crime Offenders and White Collar or Financial Offenders Act 1986 - Section 2, Telangana Prevention of Dangerous Activities of Boot-Leggers, Dacoits, Drug-Offenders, Goondas, Immoral Traffic Offenders Land-Grabbers, Spurious Seed Offenders, Insecticide Offenders, Fertiliser Offenders, Food Adulteration Offenders, Fake Document Offenders, Scheduled Commodities Offenders, Forest Offenders, Gaming Offenders, Sexual Offenders, Explosive Substances Offenders, Arms Offenders, Cyber Crime Offenders and White Collar or Financial Offenders Act 1986 - Section 3, Telangana Prevention of Dangerous Activities of Boot-Leggers, Dacoits, Drug-Offenders, Goondas, Immoral Traffic Offenders Land-Grabbers, Spurious Seed Offenders, Insecticide Offenders, Fertiliser Offenders, Food Adulteration Offenders, Fake Document Offenders, Scheduled Commodities Offenders, Forest Offenders, Gaming Offenders, Sexual Offenders, Explosive Substances Offenders, Arms Offenders, Cyber Crime Offenders and White Collar or Financial Offenders Act 1986 - Section 3(1), Telangana Prevention of Dangerous Activities of Boot-Leggers, Dacoits, Drug-Offenders, Goondas, Immoral Traffic Offenders Land-Grabbers, Spurious Seed Offenders, Insecticide Offenders, Fertiliser Offenders, Food Adulteration Offenders, Fake Document Offenders, Scheduled Commodities Offenders, Forest Offenders, Gaming Offenders, Sexual Offenders, Explosive Substances Offenders, Arms Offenders, Cyber Crime Offenders and White Collar or Financial Offenders Act 1986 - Section 3(2), Telangana Prevention of Dangerous Activities of Boot-Leggers, Dacoits, Drug-Offenders, Goondas, Immoral Traffic Offenders Land-Grabbers, Spurious Seed Offenders, Insecticide

Offenders, Fertiliser Offenders, Food Adulteration Offenders, Fake Document Offenders, Scheduled Commodities Offenders, Forest Offenders, Gaming Offenders, Sexual Offenders, Explosive Substances Offenders, Arms Offenders, Cyber Crime Offenders and White Collar or Financial Offenders Act 1986 - Section 3(3), Telangana Prevention of Dangerous Activities of Boot-Leggers, Dacoits, Drug-Offenders, Goondas, Immoral Traffic Offenders Land-Grabbers, Spurious Seed Offenders, Insecticide Offenders, Fertiliser Offenders, Food Adulteration Offenders, Fake Document Offenders, Scheduled Commodities Offenders, Forest Offenders, Gaming Offenders, Sexual Offenders, Explosive Substances Offenders, Arms Offenders, Cyber Crime Offenders and White Collar or Financial Offenders Act 1986 - Section 11

No. of pages of the Original Judgement: 11

Citation: (2020)13SCC632, MANU/SC/1781/2019

Case Note: Criminal - Detention order - Quashing of - Appellant was detained on premise that dangerous activities of offender and his associates were stated to have caused panic and feeling of insecurity in minds of general public - Brother of Appellant filed writ petition challenging order of detention - High Court dismissed Writ Petition challenging order of detention - Hence, present appeal - Whether detention order liable to be set aside.

Facts: The Appellant was detained under the provisions of Sub-section 2 of Section 3 of the Telangana Offenders Act 1986. The order of detention thereafter proceeds to state that the Appellant was implicated in Crime which was under investigation. The dangerous activities of the offender and his associates were stated to have caused panic and a feeling of insecurity in the minds of the general public. The brother of the Appellant filed a Writ Petition challenging the order of detention. On appeal, the High Court dismissed the Writ Petition challenging the order of detention.

Hon'ble Apex Court Held, while allowing the appeal: (i) The detention order had to be set aside on the grounds that reference to stale and irrelevant grounds in the detention order by the detaining authority and the manner in which the order of confirmation was presented before this Court, casts doubt on the existence of the order of confirmation in the first place. As regards the registration of Crime, the Appellant was released on bail consequent upon the failure of the investigating authority to file a charge-sheet within ninety days. A charge-sheet, had not been filed till date. There was no reasonable basis on which the detaining authority could have come to a conclusion that on being released on bail, the Appellant would in all probability indulge in prejudicial activity and it was necessary to detain him, to prevent him from engaging in prejudicial activity.

CHAPTER SIX

Ankita Kailash Khandelwal and Ors. Vs. State of Maharashtra and Ors., 2020

Hon'ble Judges/Coram: U.U. Lalit, Vineet Saran and Ajay Rastogi, JJ.

Act/ Sections: Code of Criminal Procedure, 1973 (CrPC) - Section 164, Code of Criminal Procedure, 1973 (CrPC) - Section 174, Code of Criminal Procedure, 1973 (CrPC) - Section 207, Code of Criminal Procedure, 1973 (CrPC) - Section 208, Code of Criminal Procedure, 1973 (CrPC) - Section 437(3), Code of Criminal Procedure, 1973 (CrPC) - Section 438, Code of Criminal Procedure, 1973 (CrPC) - Section 438(1), Code of Criminal Procedure, 1973 (CrPC) - Section 438(2); Constitution of India - Article 21; Indian Penal Code, 1860 (IPC) - Section 34, Indian Penal Code, 1860 (IPC) - Section 302, Indian Penal Code, 1860 (IPC) - Section 306, Indian Penal Code, 1860 (IPC) - Section 307; Information Technology Act, 2000 - Section 67; Maharashtra Medical Council Act, 1965 - Section 22(1); Maharashtra Prohibition Of Ragging Act, 1999 - Section 4, Maharashtra Prohibition Of Ragging Act, 1999 - Section 5, Maharashtra Prohibition Of Ragging Act, 1999 - Section 6, Maharashtra Prohibition Of Ragging Act, 1999 - Section 6(1); Medical Council of India (Prevention and Prohibition of Ragging in Medical Colleges/Institutions) Regulations, 2009; Medical Council of India Post Graduate Medical Education Regulations, 2000; Scheduled Castes And The Scheduled Tribes (prevention Of Atrocities) Act, 1989 - Section 3(10), Scheduled Castes And The Scheduled Tribes (prevention Of Atrocities) Act, 1989 - Section 14A, Scheduled Castes And The Scheduled Tribes (prevention Of Atrocities) Act, 1989 - Section 14A(2).

No. of pages of the Original Judgement: 15

Citation: AIR2020SC4874, (2020)10SCC670, MANU/SC/0744/2020

Case Note: Criminal - Bail - Granted subject to Conditions - Section 438 of the Code of Criminal Procedure, 1973 - Offence committed punishable under Sections 306 read with Section 34 of the Indian Penal Code, 1860 (IPC), Scheduled Caste and Scheduled Tribe (Prevention of Atrocities), Act, 1989 and Section 4 of the Maharashtra Prohibition of Ragging Act, 1999 (1999 Act) - Deceased, junior student to Appellants committed suicide - Compliant alleged Appellants of harassing deceased and directly behind death of deceased - Impugned order while granting bail imposed several conditions - Out of these three sought to be relaxed - High Court relaxed two and relaxation of one condition is sought before this Court - Whether condition to the effect of suspending Appellants from attending institution violates Article 21 of the Constitution of India, 1950?

Facts: The Appellants after completing MBBS course were pursuing Post Graduate Degree course and were working as residents in a Hospital. Deceased, a year junior to the Appellants were residents in the same Department and pursuing the same course. Police received an information that deceased had committed suicide by hanging herself in her room. Mother of deceased alleged harassment by the Appellants and they were accused of directly responsible for the suicide committed by her daughter. Case under Section 306 read with Section 34 of the Indian Penal Code, 1860 (IPC) and provisions of Scheduled Caste and Scheduled Tribe (Prevention of Atrocities), Act, 1989 and Section 4 of the Maharashtra Prohibition of Ragging Act, 1999 ('1999 Act') was registered. Appellants were suspended and they were also later arrested. Bail Application preferred by them was rejected by the Court of Sessions. High Court in appeal granted the bail subject to stringent conditions. Issue raised for adjudication was whether Appellants had the intention to drive Deceased to commit suicide.

Hon'ble Apex Court Held, while allowing the Appeals: i. Relaxation sought in respect of condition No. iv takes within its fold all submissions with respect to matters arising from the registration of the crime and steps undertaken pursuant thereto. Since the Order of Suspension was passed purely as a result of registration of crime and did not have any roots in statutory powers conferred Under Section 6 of 1999 Act, this Court can certainly grant redress to the Appellants.

ii. While balancing the competing claims, the Appellants must be allowed to go back to their courses of study otherwise the pendency of prosecution against them will add further penalty in the form of prejudicing their career. Any such adverse impact will negate their rights under Article 21 of the Constitution.

iii. Considering the matter in its entirety and especially when the Appellants have to undergo training under the same guide and in the same institution where they were registered, ends of justice would be met if condition No. (iv) as laid down by the High Court is relaxed and the Appellants are permitted to go back to the College and the Hospital to pursue their studies, subject to the following conditions: i) The Appellants shall not, in any manner, influence or even attempt to influence any of the witnesses; ii) The Appellants shall present themselves on each of the dates that the matter gets posted before the Trial Court, unless their presence is specifically exempted; iii) If it is permissible, and subject to the appropriate permission from the Dean of the College and the Hospital, the Appellants may not reside in the quarters allocated to the residents in the College and the Hospital. However, if the registration as Post Graduate students requires the Appellants to be full time residents in the College and the Hospital, then the Appellants shall do so; iv) The Appellants shall avail study leave so that their actual period of stay inside the College and the Hospital gets reduced to the maximum possible level; v) If there be any holiday or vacation and it is permissible for the residents to be outside the College and the Hospital, the Appellants shall avail that and keep themselves away from the Hospital and the College; vi) If there be any untoward incident or even likelihood of such incident, the concerned authorities shall immediately report to the Police Station of the area and ensure that the life and liberty of everyone including the Appellants are well protected.

iv. Subject to the conditions above, the Appellants be permitted to re-enter the College and the Hospital to pursue their courses of study.

v. The appeals stand allowed.

CHAPTER SEVEN

Abhijit Pawar Vs. Hemant Madhukar Nimbalkar and Ors., 2016

Hon'ble Judges/Coram: A.K. Sikri and Abhay Manohar Sapre, JJ.

Act/ Sections: Press and Registration of Books Act, 1861 - Section 2(1), Press and Registration of Books Act, 1861 - Section 7, Press and Registration of Books Act, 1861 - Section 177, Press and Registration of Books Act, 1861 - Section 178; Code of Criminal Procedure (Amendment) Act, 2005 - Section 19; Indian Penal Code, 1860 (IPC) - Section 34, Indian Penal Code, 1860 (IPC) - Section 500, Indian Penal Code, 1860 (IPC) - Section 501, Indian Penal Code, 1860 (IPC) - Section 502, Indian Penal Code, 1860 (IPC) - Section 504; Code of Criminal Procedure, 1973 (CrPC) - Section 2, Code of Criminal Procedure, 1973 (CrPC) - Section 190, Code of Criminal Procedure, 1973 (CrPC) - Section 190(1), Code of Criminal Procedure, 1973 (CrPC) - Section 200, Code of Criminal Procedure, 1973 (CrPC) - Section 202, Code of Criminal Procedure, 1973 (CrPC) - Section 202(1), Code of Criminal Procedure, 1973 (CrPC) - Section 203, Code of Criminal Procedure, 1973 (CrPC) - Section 204, Code of Criminal Procedure, 1973 (CrPC) - Section 482; Constitution of India - Article 19(1)

No. of pages of the Original Judgement: 12

Citation: AIR2017SC299, AIR2017SC299, (2017)3SCC528, MANU/SC/1655/2016

Case Note: Criminal - Legality of procedure - Issue of process - Police squad working under Karnataka Lokayukta - Raided house of complainant - After said raid, Lokayukta held press conference - Stated - Complainant, an IPS officer - Posted as Superintendent of Police with charge of anti-terrorist squad - Collected assets worth Rs. 250 crores - Press statement widely reported the next day - Prominent national as well as local newspapers - Sakal Newspaper, a Marathi Newspaper - Carried and published said news - Other editions also carried similar news - Kolhapur edition carried new item - Caption "Rich from Silver and Elephant Teeth Smuggling" - Another editiorial was published with caption 'Police "Dog" Millionaire' - Complainant, agitated by said publications filed complaint - Section 501, 502 and 504 read with Section 34 of Indian Penal Code - A-1-Managing Director of Sakal Newspaper and A-2-Chairman of the group of Newspapers - Also arrayed as accused persons - Trial Court issued process against all accused persons - Said order challenged by accused persons - Filed criminal revision - Sessions Court dismissed the same - As A-1 did not appear before Trial Court - Even after dismissal of criminal revision - Bailable warrants issued against him - Aggrieved, both A-1 and A-2 approached High Court - Filed criminal writ petitions - High Court dismissed the writ petition of A-1 - Allowed A-2's writ petition - A-1 filed the Criminal Appeal - Complainant filed another against quashing of proceedings against A-2 - Whether the learned Magistrate adopted the correct procedure while issuing notice to A-1 and A-2.

Facts: A police squad working under the Lokayukta of Karnataka State, raided house of Hemant Madhukar Nimbalkar (complainant). After the said raid, the Lokayukta held a press conference in which he stated that the complainant, an IPS Officer and posted as Superintendent of Police with charge of anti-terrorist squad, had collected assets worth Rs. 250 crores. The press statement issued by the Lokayukta was widely reported the very next day in a number of prominent national as well as local newspapers.

Sakal Newspaper, a Marathi newspaper also carried and published this news item. The statements given by the Lokayukta also appeared in other editions of Sakal newspaper.

Kolhapur edition also carried out another separate news item under the caption 'Rich from Silver and Elephant Teeth Smuggling' mentioning that the complainant had collected money from silver and elephant teeth smuggling which came to the knowledge of the newspaper from reliable sources. Another editorial was published in Sakal newspaper with the heading 'Police "Dog" Millionaire' reference being made to the Oscar winning movie "Slum Dog Millionaire".

The complainant, feeling agitated by the aforesaid publications, filed the complaint before the Chief Judicial Magistrate, Kolhapur Under Section 501, 502 and 504 read with Section 34 of the Indian Penal Code. In this complaint apart from the four editors of the four editions of the newspaper at Kolhapur, Belgaum, Pune and Nasik, Mr. Abhijit Pawar (A-1), Managing Director of Sakal Newspaper and Mr. Pratap Rao Govind Rao Pawar (A-2), Chairman of this group of Newspapers (who incidentally is father of Abhijit Pawar) were also arrayed as accused persons.

The Trial Court issued process against all accused persons. Being aggrieved, all the accused persons challenged that order by filing criminal revision before the Sessions Court which was dismissed by the Court of Sessions. As A-1 did not appear before the Trial Court even after the dismissal of the criminal revision application, bailable warrants were issued against him. Aggrieved, both A-1 and his father, A-2 approached the High Court by way of respective criminal writ petitions. The learned High Court dismissed the Writ petition of A-1 while allowing the writ petition of A-2. Hence, A-1 has filed the Criminal Appeal. Against the part of High Court quashing proceedings against A-2, the Complainant has filed the Criminal Appeal.

Hon'ble Apex Court Held, while allowing the appeals: Admitted position in law is that in those cases where the accused is residing at a place beyond the area in which the Magistrate exercises his jurisdiction, it is mandatory on the part of the Magistrate to conduct an enquiry or investigation before issuing the process. Section 202 of the Code of Criminal Procedure was amended in the year by the Code of Criminal Procedure (Amendment) Act, 2005, with effect from 22nd June, 2006 by adding the words 'and shall, in a case where the accused is residing at a place beyond the area in which he exercises his jurisdiction'. There is a vital purpose or objective behind this amendment, namely, to ward off false complaints against such persons residing at a far-off places in order to save them from unnecessary harassment. Thus, the amended provision casts an obligation on the Magistrate to conduct enquiry or direct investigation before issuing the process, so that false complaints are filtered and rejected. The aforesaid purpose is specifically mentioned in the note appended to the Bill proposing the said amendment.

For this reason, the amended provision casts an obligation on the Magistrate to apply his mind carefully and satisfy himself that the allegations in the complaint, when considered along with the statements recorded or the enquiry conducted thereon, would prima facie constitute the offence for which the complaint is filed.

The requirement of conducting enquiry or directing investigation before issuing process is, therefore, not an empty formality. When the Court perused the summoning order, it found that it does not reflect any such inquiry. No doubt, the order mentioned that the learned Magistrate had passed the same after reading the complaint, verification statement of complainant and after perusing the copies of documents filed on record, i.e., FIR translation of complaint, affidavit of advocate who had translated the FIR into English etc.

In so far as, these two accused persons are concerned there is no enquiry of the nature enumerated in Section 202, Code of Criminal Procedure. The Learned Magistrate did not look into the matter keeping in view the provisions of Section 7 of the Press Act and applying his mind whether there is any declaration qua these two persons under the said Act and, if not, on what basis they are to be proceeded with along with the editors. Application of mind on this aspect was necessary. It is made clear that this Court is not suggesting that these two accused persons cannot be proceeded with at all only because of absence of their names in the declaration under Press Act. What is emphasised is that there is no presumption against these persons Under Section 7 of the Press Act and they being outside the territorial jurisdiction of the concerned Magistrate, the Magistrate was required to apply his mind on these aspects while passing summoning orders qua A-1 and A-2.

No doubt, the argument predicated on Section 202 of the Code of Criminal Procedure was raised for the first time by A-1 before the High Court. Notwithstanding the same, being a pure legal issue, which could be tested on the basis of admitted facts on record, the High Court could have considered this argument on merits. It is a settled proposition of law that a pure legal issue can be raised at any stage of proceedings, more so, when it goes to the jurisdiction of the matter.

For the aforesaid reasons, Criminal Appeal arising out of SLP (Crl) No. 9318 of 2012 is allowed thereby quashing the notice dated 24th November, 2009 in respect of A-1 with direction to the learned Magistrate to take up the matter afresh qua A-1 and pass necessary orders as are permissible in law, after following the procedure contained in Section 202, Code of Criminal

Procedure.

Insofar as appeal filed by the complainant discharging A-2 is concerned, the High Court has quashed the notice on the ground that he is only shown as Chairman and is not shown to be actually associated with the publication of the newspaper. Since, the Court was relegating the matter insofar as A-1 is concerned, for the same reasons the complainant needs to be given an opportunity to show as to whether A-2 was actually associated with the publication or not. It is more so when the Court found that High Court has not given any cogent reasons on the basis of which it has said that Chairman is not shown to be associated with the impugned publication. Thus, the Court allowed the second appeal as well and directed the learned Magistrate to hold the same inquiry as directed qua A-1 and apply his mind as to whether notice against A-1 and A-2 needs to be issued or not.

CHAPTER EIGHT

Gautam Kundu Vs. Manoj Kumar, Govt. of India, 2015

Hon'ble Judges/Coram: Pinaki Chandra Ghose and R.K. Agrawal, JJ.

Act/ Sections: Companies Act, 1956 - Section 56, Companies Act, 1956 - Section 67(3), Companies Act, 1956 - Section 117A; Securities and Exchange Board of India Act, 1992 - Section 4, Securities and Exchange Board of India Act, 1992 - Section 11C, Securities and Exchange Board of India Act, 1992 - Section 11C(3), Securities and Exchange Board of India Act, 1992 - Section 12A, Securities and Exchange Board of India Act, 1992 - Section 24, Securities and Exchange Board of India Act, 1992 - Section 26; Prevention of Money-Laundering Act, 2002 - Section 2, Prevention of Money-Laundering Act, 2002 - Section 3, Prevention of Money-Laundering Act, 2002 - Section 4, Prevention of Money-Laundering Act, 2002 - Section 8, Prevention of Money-Laundering Act, 2002 - Section 8(1), Prevention of Money-Laundering Act, 2002 - Section 24, Prevention of Money-Laundering Act, 2002 - Section 44(1), Prevention of Money-Laundering Act, 2002 - Section 45, Prevention of Money-Laundering Act, 2002 - Section 45(1), Prevention of Money-Laundering Act, 2002 - Section 65, Prevention of Money-Laundering Act, 2002 - Section 71; Prevention of Money-Laundering (Amendment) Act, 2012 [Repealed]; Prevention of Money-Laundering (Amendment) Act 2009; Indian Penal Code, 1860 (IPC) - Section 405; Code of Criminal Procedure, 1973 (CrPC) - Section 5, Code of Criminal Procedure, 1973 (CrPC) - Section 439; Securities and Exchange Board of India Rules; Securities and Exchange Board of India Regulations

No. of pages of the Original Judgement: 13

Citation: AIR2016SC106, (2015)16SCC1, MANU/SC/1453/2015

Case Note: Criminal - Refusal to grant bail - Appellant - Chairman of Rose Valley - Public Company incorporated and registered under

Companies Act, 1956 - Certain non-convertible debentures issued by Rose valley - 'Private placement method' - No advertisements issued to public - Issued to employees, their friends and associates - Fulfilled formalities of private placement - Appellant collected money - Issue of debentures from time to time - Letter issued by SEBI - Informed Appellant about offences alleged to have committed by it - Appeal filed before SAT allowed - Held - Appellant Company had repaid all money collected from investors - Further held - No grounds for violation of Section 11(C)(3) of SEBI Act - Report filed by Respondent - Alleged commission of offence under Section 24 of SEBI Act - Proceedings challenged in High Court - Pending for hearing - SEBI directed Appellant to refund money to customers of Ashirbad scheme - Order challenged before SAT - Show Cause Notice under Section 8(1) of PMLA served - Appellant filed writ petition before High Court - Challenged notice - Dismissed - Appeal to Division Bench - Dismissed - Division Bench directed Appellant to appear before Adjudicating Authority - Authority to pass a reasoned order - Complaint filed by Respondent in Court of learned Chief Judge, City Sessions Court - Under Section 4 of PMLA - Appellant arrested on suspicion of commission of offence punishable under provisions of PMLA - Detained in custody since - Appellant - Granted bail of father's death - Surrendered later - Filed a fresh bail application - Section 439 of Code of Criminal Procedure - High Court rejected said application - Present Appeal -Whether the provisions of Section 45 of the PMLA are binding on the High Court while considering the application for bail Under Section 439 of the Code of Criminal Procedure - Whether the High Court has exercised its discretion under Section 439 of Code of Criminal Procedure, 1973 capriciously or arbitrarily by refusing bail to the Appellant.

Facts: The Appellant is the Chairman of Rose Valley Real Estate Construction Ltd. (Rose Valley), a public company incorporated in 1999 and registered under the Companies Act, 1956. Certain non-convertible debentures were issued by the Rose Valley by 'private placement method.' No advertisements etc. were issued to the public. The said debentures were issued to the employees of the Company and to their friends and associates after fulfilling the formalities for private placement of debentures. Thus, the Appellant collected money by issuing secured debentures by way of private placement in compliance with the guidelines issued by the Securities and Exchange Board of India (SEBI) from time to time.

In 2013, the Adjudicating Officer, SEBI, passed an order imposing a penalty of Rs. 1 crore upon the Rose Valley for violation of the provisions of

Sections 11(C) of the Securities and Exchange Board of India Act, 1992 (the SEBI Act) which was reduced to Rs. 10 lakhs by the Securities Appellate Tribunal. A letter was issued by SEBI to the Appellant informing about the offences alleged to have been committed by it under the Companies Act, SEBI Act & Regulations, and Section 405 of the Indian Penal Code, 1860. The appeal filed by the Appellant before the Securities Appellate Tribunal was allowed holding that the Appellant Company has repaid all the money collected from the investors. It was further held by the Securities Appellate Tribunal that there are no grounds for violation of Section 11(C)(3) of the SEBI Act.

On basis of letter issued by SEBI, the Respondent filed a report, alleging commission of offence by the Rose Valley and its officers, punishable Under Section 24 of the SEBI Act. A complaint was filed by the Respondent authorities, alleging that the Rose Valley transferred the money raised by issue of debentures from the account of one company to that of another company. It is also alleged that the money collected by issuing the debentures for the purpose of one business has been invested in some other business. The proceedings Under Section 24 of the SEBI Act have been challenged in the High Court by way of revision which is pending for hearing and further proceeding of the complaint case, has been stayed by the High Court. The High Court also directed the Respondent not to take any coercive measure against the Appellant.

Vide its order, SEBI directed Appellant Rose Valley to refund the money to the customers of Ashirbad scheme. This order was challenged before the Securities Appellate Tribunal by way of appeal. A Show Cause Notice Under Section 8(1) of the Prevention of Money Laundering Act, 2002 (PMLA) was served upon Rose Valley and its officials. Rose Valley filed a writ petition before the High Court challenging the said Show Cause Notice. The said writ petition was dismissed by the learned Single Judge of the High Court. Thereafter, the matter was taken in appeal before the Division Bench. The Division Bench dismissed the said appeal and directed the Appellant Rose Valley to appear before the Adjudicating Authority Under Section 8 of the PMLA and directed the Adjudicating Authority to decide the preliminary objections as may be raised by the Rose Valley, including the applicability of the PMLA as also the validity of the search and seizure against Rose Valley. It was further directed that the Adjudicating Authority should pass a reasoned order in the matter and communicate the same to the Appellant.

A complaint was filed by the Respondent in the Court of learned Chief Judge, City Sessions Court against the Appellant Under Section 4 of PMLA, though no offence is made out against the Appellant Under Section 3 of the PMLA. Despite having fully cooperated with the investigation, the Appellant was arrested on suspicion of having committed an offence punishable under the provisions of the PMLA and is detained in custody since then.

While the Appellant was in custody, his father expired upon which he moved an application before the High Court for interim bail to perform the rituals for his deceased father. The High Court directed release of the Appellant on provisional bail for two weeks on the conditions mentioned in the said order. On completion of the period of provisional bail, the Appellant duly surrendered before the Court of learned Chief Judge, City Sessions Court.

In July 2015, Appellant filed a fresh bail application under Section 439 of the Code of Criminal Procedure before the High Court. Vide impugned judgment and order the High Court has rejected the said application of the Appellant holding that no order has yet been passed by any competent Court of law that no offence is made out against the Appellant Under Section 24 of the SEBI Act. A criminal revision praying for quashing of the proceedings initiated against the Appellant Under Section 24 of the SEBI Act is still pending for decision before the High Court. Aggrieved by the rejection of the bail application filed Under Section 439 of the Code of Criminal Procedure, the Appellant has approached this Court through this appeal by special leave.

Hon'ble Apex Court Held, while dismissing the appeal: 1. There is no doubt that PMLA deals with the offence of money laundering and the Parliament has enacted this law as per commitment of the country to the United Nations General Assembly. PMLA is a special statute enacted by the Parliament for dealing with money laundering. Section 5 of the Code of Criminal Procedure, 1973 clearly lays down that the provisions of the Code of Criminal Procedure will not affect any special statute or any local law. In other words, the provisions of any special statute will prevail over the general provisions of the Code of Criminal Procedure in case of any conflict.

2. The conditions specified Under Section 45 of the PMLA are mandatory and needs to be complied with which is further strengthened by the provisions of Section 65 and also Section 71 of the PMLA. Section 65 requires that the provisions of Code of Criminal Procedure shall apply in so far as they are not inconsistent with the provisions of this Act and Section 71 provides that the provisions of the PMLA shall have overriding effect notwithstanding anything inconsistent therewith contained in any other law for the time being in force. PMLA has an overriding effect and the provisions of Code of Criminal Procedure would apply only if they are not inconsistent with the provisions of this Act. Therefore, the conditions enumerated in Section 45 of PMLA will have to be complied with even in respect of an application for bail made Under Section 439 of Code of Criminal Procedure That coupled with the provisions of Section 24 provides that unless the contrary is proved, the Authority or the Court shall presume that proceeds of crime are involved in money laundering and the burden to prove that the proceeds of crime are not involved, lies on the Appellant.

3. The Court refrained itself from deciding the questions tried to be raised since it is nothing but a bail application. The Court did not forget that this case is relating to "Money Laundering" which it feels is a serious threat to the national economy and national interest. The Court could not brush aside the fact that the schemes have been prepared in a calculative manner with a deliberative design and motive of personal gain, regardless of the consequence to the members of the society.

4. With regard to the questions raised by learned senior Counsel appearing on behalf of the Appellant, at this stage, the Court did not think that it should answer or deal with the same in view of the fact that the matter is pending before a Division Bench of the High Court in writ jurisdiction. Hence, any observation or remarks made by the Court may cause prejudice to the case of both the sides. Therefore, the Court felt that it would be proper for it only to deal with the matter concerning bail.

5. The Court noted that admittedly the complaint is filed against the Appellant on the allegations of committing the offence punishable Under Section 4 of the PMLA. The contention raised on behalf of the Appellant that no offence Under Section 24 of the SEBI Act is made out against the Appellant, which is a scheduled offence under the PMLA, needs to be considered from the materials collected during the investigation by the Respondents. There is no order as yet passed by a competent court of law, holding that no offence is made out against the Appellant Under Section 24

of the SEBI Act and it would be noteworthy that a criminal revision praying for quashing the proceedings initiated against the Appellant Under Section 24 of SEBI Act is still pending for hearing before the High Court.

6. The Court further noted that Section 45 of the PMLA will have overriding effect on the general provisions of the Code of Criminal Procedure in case of conflict between them. Section 45 of the PMLA imposes two conditions for grant of bail, specified under the said Act. The Court has not missed the proviso to Section 45 of the said Act which indicates that the legislature has carved out an exception for grant of bail by a Special Court when any person is under the age of 16 years or is a woman or is a sick or infirm. Therefore, there is no doubt that the conditions laid down Under Section 45A of the PMLA, would bind the High Court as the provisions of special law having overriding effect on the provisions of Section 439 of the Code of Criminal Procedure for grant of bail to any person accused of committing offence punishable Under Section 4 of the PMLA, even when the application for bail is considered Under Section 439 of the Code of Criminal Procedure.

7. The Court could not brush aside the fact that the Appellant floated as many as 27 companies to allure the investors to invest in their different companies on a promise of high returns and funds were collected from the public at large which were subsequently laundered in associated companies of Rose Valley Group and were used for purchasing moveable and immoveable properties.

8. The Court did not intend to further state the other facts excepting the fact that admittedly the complaint was filed against the Appellant on the allegation of committing offence punishable Under Section 4 of the PMLA. The contention made on behalf of the Appellant that no offence Under Section 24 of the SEBI Act is made out against the Appellant, which is a scheduled offence under the PMLA, needs to be considered from the material collected during the investigation and further to be considered by the competent court of law. The Court did not intend to express itself at this stage with regard to the same as it may cause prejudice the case of the parties in other proceedings. The Court was sure that it is not expected at this stage that the guilt of the accused has to be established beyond reasonable doubt through evidences.

9. The Court further noted that the High Court at the time of refusing

the bail application, duly considered this fact and further considered the statement of the Assistant General Manager of RBI, Kolkata, seizure list, statements of directors of Rose Valley, statements of officer bearers of Rose Valley, statements of debenture trustees of Rose Valley, statements of debenture holders of Rose Valley, statements of AGM of Accounts of Rose Valley and statements of Regional Managers of Rose Valley for formation of opinion whether the Appellant is involved in the offence of money laundering.

10. In these circumstances, the Court did not find that the High Court exercised its discretion capriciously or arbitrarily in the facts and circumstances of this case. It further noted that the High Court had called for all the relevant papers and duly taken note of that and thereafter after satisfying its conscience, refused the bail. Therefore, the Court did not find that the High Court had committed any wrong in refusing bail in the given circumstances. Accordingly, Court did not find any reason to interfere with the impugned order so passed by the High Court and the bail, as prayed before it, challenging the said order was refused. Consequently, the appeal is dismissed.

CHAPTER NINE

State of Odisha Vs. Pratima Mohanty and Ors., 2021

Hon'ble Judges/Coram: M.R. Shah and B.V. Nagarathna, JJ.

Act/ Sections: Code of Criminal Procedure, 1973 (CrPC) - Section 155(2), Code of Criminal Procedure, 1973 (CrPC) - Section 156(1), Code of Criminal Procedure, 1973 (CrPC) - Section 482; Indian Penal Code, 1860 (IPC) - Section 120B, Indian Penal Code, 1860 (IPC) - Section 420; Prevention of Corruption Act, 1988 - Section 13(1), Prevention of Corruption Act, 1988 - Section 13(2)

No. of pages of the Original Judgement: 09

Citation: AIR2022SC41, MANU/SC/1223/2021

Case Note: Criminal - Quashing of Proceedings - Criminal conspiracy - Misuse of official position - Section 13(2) read with Section 13(1)(d) of the Prevention of Corruption Act, 1988 and Section 420 read with Section 120B of the Indian Penal Code, 1860 (IPC) - Section 482 of the Code of Criminal Procedure, 1973 - Allotment of plots allegedly made by Respondent-Accused arbitrarily and to family members - Charge sheet filed by Vigilance Cell - High Court vide impugned judgment quashed proceedings - Hence, the present appeal - Whether High Court erred in quashing criminal proceedings against Accused/ Respondents for want of material against them?

Facts: In the present case allegations were made with respect to allotment of 10 plots which were required to be allotted under the discretionary quota. At the relevant time, the Respondents - Accused were connected with the Department concerned with regard to allotment of the plots directly or indirectly. The accused were alleged of misusing their official position and thereby causing loss to public exchequer.

Hon'ble Apex Court Held, while allowing the Appeal: Looking to the allegations in the present case against the Respondents - Accused and considering the fact that charge-sheet has been filed by the Vigilance Cell after a thorough investigation, it cannot be said that the case falls within any of the exceptions as carved out. It cannot be said that the criminal proceedings initiated against the Respondents - Accused are an abuse of process of any court. On the contrary, the allegations are an instance of abuse of the powers with a mala fide intention and allotment of the plots to the family members by hatching a criminal conspiracy and to allot the plots to the family members at throw away price causing loss to the B.D.A. and the public exchequer.

It is trite that the power of quashing should be exercised sparingly and with circumspection and in rare cases. Normally the criminal proceedings should not be quashed in exercise of powers under Section 482 Code of Criminal Procedure when after a thorough investigation the charge-sheet has been filed. At the stage of discharge and/or considering the application Under Section 482 Code of Criminal Procedure the courts are not required to go into the merits of the allegations and/or evidence in detail as if conducing the mini-trial.

It cannot be said that the criminal proceedings against the Respondents - Accused were in any way an abuse of process of law and/or the Court. The allegations against the Respondents - Accused are very serious including hatching a criminal conspiracy in allotment of 10 plots in the discretionary quota arbitrarily and to their own family members/relatives.

While quashing the criminal proceedings the High Court has embarked upon an enquiry as to the reliability and genuineness of the evidence collected during the investigation as if the High Court was conducting the mini-trial. Appeals succeed. Impugned common judgment and order passed quashed and set aside in so far as quashing the criminal proceedings against original Accused Nos. 4, 5 & 3 is concerned.

CHAPTER TEN

The State of Jammu & Kashmir and Ors. Vs. Saleem Ur Rehman, 2021

Hon'ble Judges/Coram: M.R. Shah and A.S. Bopanna, JJ.

Act/ Sections: Code of Criminal Procedure, 1973 (CrPC) - Section 56, Code of Criminal Procedure, 1973 (CrPC) - Section 154, Code of Criminal Procedure, 1973 (CrPC) - Section 155, Code of Criminal Procedure, 1973 (CrPC) - Section 155(1), Code of Criminal Procedure, 1973 (CrPC) - Section 155(4), Code of Criminal Procedure, 1973 (CrPC) - Section 156(1), Code of Criminal Procedure, 1973 (CrPC) - Section 156(2), Code of Criminal Procedure, 1973 (CrPC) - Section 156(3), Code of Criminal Procedure, 1973 (CrPC) - Section 173; Code of Criminal Procedure (CrPC), Samvat 1989 - Section 56, Code of Criminal Procedure (CrPC), Samvat 1989 - Section 155; Constitution of India - Article 226, Constitution of India - Article 227; Indian Penal Code, 1860 (IPC) - Section 161, Indian Penal Code, 1860 (IPC) - Section 165, Indian Penal Code, 1860 (IPC) - Section 165A; Jammu and Kashmir Prevention of Corruption Act, 1949 - Section 3, Jammu and Kashmir Prevention of Corruption Act, 1949 - Section 5(1), Jammu and Kashmir Prevention of Corruption Act, 1949 - Section 5(2); Jammu and Kashmir Vigilance Manual, 2008 - Rule 3.16; Prevention Of Corruption Act, 1947 - Section 3, Prevention Of Corruption Act, 1947 - Section 5, Prevention Of Corruption Act, 1947 - Section 5A, Prevention Of Corruption Act, 1947 - Section 5(1), Prevention Of Corruption Act, 1947 - Section 5A(1), Prevention Of Corruption Act, 1947 - Section 5(2), Prevention Of Corruption Act, 1947 - Section 5(4); Prevention Of Corruption Act, 1988 - Section 13, Prevention Of Corruption Act, 1988 -

Section 13(1), Prevention Of Corruption Act, 1988 - Section 17, Prevention Of Corruption Act, 1988 - Section 23(2), Prevention of Corruption Act, 1988 - Section 5A; Ranbir Penal Code, 1989 - Section 120B

No. of pages of the Original Judgement: 17

Citation: MANU/SC/1022/2021

Case Note: Criminal - Quashing of proceedings -FIR registered under Section 5(1)(d) read with 5(2) of the J&K Prevention of Corruption Act, 2006 (J&K PC Act) - Section 120B of the Ranbir Penal Code (RPC) -Respondent alleged of misappropriation of government money by effecting purchases of sub-standard medical kits at highly exorbitant rates - High Court by impugned judgment quashed criminal proceedings and declared Rule 3.16 of the Vigilance Manual, 2008 in direct conflict with the Constitution Bench Judgment in the case of Lalita Kumari v. Government of Uttar Pradesh - Subject provision declared ultra vires - Hence, the present appeal by State - Whether High Court by impugned judgment erred in quashing proceedings and declaring Rule 3.16 of the Vigilance Manual, 2008 ultravires?

Facts: In the instead case, FIR was registered against the Respondent alleging that during 2010-11, the Director Health Services, Kashmir along with the other Accused persons misappropriated the huge amount of government money by way of effecting purchases of sub-standard medical kits under National Rural Health Mission (NRHM) at highly exorbitant rates and in violation of the conditions of supply orders placed by the department. High Court vide impugned judgment quashed entire proceedings and hence the present appeal.

Hon'ble Apex Court Held, while allowing the Appeal: Offence under the Prevention of Corruption Act is a substantive offence and the investigation in respect of the offence under the PC Act, when considered and coupled with the offence of conspiracy, there is no requirement of prior sanction of the Magistrate. Merely because the offence of the conspiracy may be involved, investigation into the substantive offence, i.e., in the present case, offence under the PC Act which is cognizable is not required to await a sanction from the Magistrate, as that would lead to a considerable delay and affect the investigation and it will derail the investigation. Therefore, the High Court has erred in quashing the criminal proceedings on the ground that as the offence under Section 120B which is a non-cognizable, prior sanction as required under Section 155 of J&K Code of Criminal Procedure is not obtained.

As per Clause 3.16 only after the Preliminary Enquiry is conducted and there is a prima facie case found, an FIR is required to be registered. Considering the nature of offences, a detailed enquiry is required and therefore it is observed in Clause 3.16 that a PE should be completed normally within a period of six months. It is the case on behalf of the Respondent and even as observed and held by the High Court in the impugned judgment and order as per the law laid down by this Court in the case of Lalita Kumari, a detailed investigation into the allegations on merits is not required by holding Preliminary Enquiry and that such enquiry is to be completed within a period of 7 days is concerned, it is to be noted that in the case of LalitaKumari, it is not held that if the Preliminary Enquiry is not completed within a period of 7 days, the entire criminal proceedings would be void and the same are to be quashed.

While holding a Preliminary Enquiry under Clause 3.16, whatever is conducted will be in the form of enquiry into the allegations to consider whether any prima facie case is made out or not which requires further investigation after registering the FIR or not. While considering the prima facie case for the purpose of registering the FIR, some enquiry/investigation is bound to be there, however, the same shall be only for the purpose of finding out a prima facie case for the purpose of registration of the FIR only. Merely because while holding a Preliminary Enquiry a detailed enquiry is made into the allegations made against the Respondent which, as observed hereinabove, can be said to be only for the purpose of finding out a prima facie case for the purpose of registration of the FIR and merely because some more time is taken in conducting the Preliminary Enquiry before registering the FIR, the entire criminal proceedings cannot be quashed. High Court has materially erred in holding and declaring Clause 3.16 as ultra vires.

Impugned judgment and order passed by the High Court quashing the entire criminal proceedings and quashing and setting aside the Entrustment Order authorising the Inspector to investigate the FIR and holding and declaring Rule/Clause 3.16 of the Vigilance Manual, 2008 dealing with Preliminary Enquiry (PE) as ultra vires is unsustainable and thus quashed and set aside.

Appeal allowed.

CHAPTER ELEVEN

Narendra Kumar A. Baldota Vs. The State of Karnataka, 2022

Hon'ble Judges/Coram: Indira Banerjee and J.K. Maheshwari, JJ.

Act/ Sections: Code of Criminal Procedure, 1973 (CrPC) - Section 156(3), Code of Criminal Procedure, 1973 (CrPC) - Section 200, Code of Criminal Procedure, 1973 (CrPC) - Section 482; Constitution of India - Article 226; Indian Penal Code, 1860 (IPC) - Section 34, Indian Penal Code, 1860 (IPC) - Section 120B, Indian Penal Code, 1860 (IPC) - Section 406, Indian Penal Code, 1860 (IPC) - Section 420, Indian Penal Code, 1860 (IPC) - Section 427, Indian Penal Code, 1860 (IPC) - Section 447, Indian Penal Code, 1860 (IPC) - Section 506; Karnataka Motor Vehicles Taxation Act, 1957 - Section 8(a), Karnataka Motor Vehicles Taxation Act, 1957 - Section 8A, Karnataka Motor Vehicles Taxation Act, 1957 - Section 21; Negotiable Instruments Act, 1881 - Section 138; Prevention Of Corruption Act, 1988 - Section 13(1), Prevention Of Corruption Act, 1988 - Section 13(2), Prevention Of Corruption Act, 1988 - Section 17

No. of pages of the Original Judgement: 11

Citation: MANU/SC/0799/2022

Case Note: Criminal - Quashing of proceedings - Sections 13(1)(c) and 13(1)(d) read with Section 13(2) of the Prevention of Corruption Act, 1988 ("the P.C. Act") and Sections 120B and 420 of the Indian Penal Code, 1860 ("IPC") - Present Appeal is against an order passed by the High Court dismissing the Criminal Petition filed by the Appellant under Section 482 of the Code of Criminal Procedure, 1973 ("Cr.P.C."), seeking to quash the proceedings against the Appellant for offences punishable under Sections

13(1)(c) and 13(1)(d) read with Section 13(2) of the P.C. Act and Sections 120B and 420 of the IPC - Whether proceedings against the Appellant are misconceived?

Facts: The Appellant is the Chairman and Managing Director of MSPL Limited. In 2010, MSPL Limited imported an Aston Martin Rapide car for which the Company paid the applicable customs duty. The Company also paid road tax to the Regional Transport Office (RTO), Hosapete. One Jagadish B.N., Advocate filed a private complaint in the Court of XXIII Additional City Civil Sessions Judge, alleging that there was collusion and conspiracy between RTOs in Karnataka as a result of which appropriate road tax was not being collected. It was alleged that cars were being imported in Karnataka for which RTO was not charging road tax as per the actual cost. The complainant claims that the vehicle dealers, middle man, smugglers across the country and owners of the imported vehicle at Mangalore have misquoted and collected the price of Bentley and Ferrari car have come away with the registration, and in the process have also managed suppress the brand names of the cars. The complainant claims that he is unable to procure that facts which have been hidden and buried at high public functionaries and it is only an authorised investigating agency that can unearth the fraud taken place regarding the fraud in the registration. By an order, the learned III Additional District and Sessions Judge, took cognizance, and issued summons to the Appellant. Thereafter, the Appellant filed Criminal Petition before the High Court praying that the proceedings on the file of the III Additional District and Sessions Judge, be quashed as against the Appellant. High Court dismissed the petition.

Hon'ble Apex Court Held, while allowing the appeal: 1. Appellant is Chairman and Managing Director of the corporate entity, which purchased the vehicle in question. There is not a whisper in the chargesheet of the specific role played by the Appellant or how he committed the offence of cheating.

2. Criminal law cannot be set into motion as a matter of course. Summoning of an Accused in a criminal case is a serious matter. To set Criminal law into motion, the order of the Magistrate summoning the Accused, must reflect that he has applied his mind to the facts of the case. Before the Magistrate issues summons to a Chairman, Managing Director, Director or any other official of the company, the Magistrate has to record his satisfaction of a prima facie case against him/her in his/her own capacity is sine qua non for initiation of criminal proceedings against a

Chairman, Managing Director or officer of a company. It is well settled that no official of a company can be dragged into criminal proceedings only in his/her capacity as official of the company, without any specific role attributed to him/her in relation to the offence alleged against the company.

3. The Appellant claims that he has never been involved in any criminal offence in his life time. The false implication of the Appellant would damage the reputation of the Appellant. There being absolutely no materials against the Appellant anywhere in the chargesheet, the proceedings as against the Appellant are liable to be quashed. The filing of the chargesheet against the Appellant is arbitrary, harassive and unsupported by any materials on record.

4. The Appellant has not questioned initiation of criminal proceedings against any of the other Accused persons. He has no intention of stalling proceedings against any person involved in smuggling cars or forging or fabricating documents or committing any other illegal activities. He has questioned the legality of initiation of proceedings against him for alleged short payment of road tax in respect of a vehicle owned by the company of which he is Chairman and Managing Director even though, the alleged deficit road tax had been paid by the company within one month of issuance of demand notice.

5. There is no whisper of how and in what manner the Appellant has abetted the commission of any offence. It is nobody's case that any document submitted in connection with the vehicle in question imported by M/s. MSPL Limited is fake or fabricated. That is not the charge, so far as the Appellant is concerned. From Paragraph 11 of the order dated 7th August 2012, it transpires that in case of some of the cars, the owners had declared the selling rates at the factory as the value of the car, and not the on-road value which would be about three times the factory value.

6. The mere fact that demand notice may have been issued and the differential tax realized before institution of the private complaint is inconsequential. Either the charges disclose an offence of defrauding the State of revenue or the offence of defrauding the State of revenue not made out. The question is whether the materials on record disclose any criminal act on the part of these Appellants. The answer cannot but be in the negative.

7. Proceedings against the Appellant are misconceived, harassive, in abuse of process of law and have been initiated without proper application

of mind. Appeal allowed.

CHAPTER TWELVE

Central Bureau of Investigation and Ors. Vs. Thommandru Hannah Vijayalakshmi and Ors., 2021

Hon'ble Judges/Coram: Dr. D.Y. Chandrachud, Vikram Nath and B.V. Nagarathna, JJ.

Act/ Sections: Central Civil Services (Conduct) Rules 1964; Code of Criminal Procedure, 1973 (CrPC) - Section 91, Code of Criminal Procedure, 1973 (CrPC) - Section 154, Code of Criminal Procedure, 1973 (CrPC) - Section 155(2), Code of Criminal Procedure, 1973 (CrPC) - Section 156(1), Code of Criminal Procedure, 1973 (CrPC) - Section 160, Code of Criminal Procedure, 1973 (CrPC) - Section 173, Code of Criminal Procedure, 1973 (CrPC) - Section 438, Code of Criminal Procedure, 1973 (CrPC) - Section 482; Constitution of India - Article 32, Constitution of India - Article 226; Delhi Special Police Establishment Act, 1946 - Section 3, Delhi Special Police Establishment Act, 1946 - Section 5, Delhi Special Police Establishment Act, 1946 - Section 6; Indian Evidence Act, 1872 - Section 43; Indian Penal Code, 1860 (IPC) - Section 109; Prevention of Corruption (Amendment) Act, 2018; Prevention Of Corruption Act, 1947 - Section 5(1), Prevention Of Corruption Act, 1988 - Section 13(1), Prevention Of Corruption Act, 1988 - Section 13(2); Representation of the People Act 1951; Scheduled Cases and Scheduled Tribes (Prevention of Atrocities) Act 1989

No. of pages of the Original Judgement: 29

Citation: AIR2021SC5041, MANU/SC/0831/2021

Case Note: Criminal - Quashing of FIR - Possession of Disproportionate Assets - Section 13(2) read with Section 13(1)(e) of the Prevention of Corruption Act 1988 and Section 109 of the Indian Penal Code 1860 - High Court quashed the FIR finding allegations levelled unstainable - Hence, the present appeal - Whether the CBI is mandatorily required to conduct a Preliminary Enquiry before the registration of an FIR in every case involving claims of alleged corruption against public servants? - Whether the judgment of the High Court to quash the FIR can be sustained in the present case?

Facts: The present appeal was preferred against the judgment whereby writ petition filed by the Respondents was allowed and First Information Report registered against the Respondents was set aside, together with proceedings taken up pursuant to the FIR. R1 is a Commissioner of Income Tax while R2 is her spouse and Member of the Legislative Assembly and is a Minister in the State government of Andhra Pradesh. The FIR was registered against the R1 for being in possession (allegedly) of assets disproportionate to her known sources of income. R2 was alleged to have abetted the offence. The FIR was registered for offences punishable under Section 13(2) read with Section 13(1)(e) of the Prevention of Corruption Act 1988 and Section 109 of the Indian Penal Code 1860. High Court had held that on the basis of the information ascertained from the 'known sources of income', the allegations against the Respondents in the FIR prima facie were unsustainable.

Hon'ble Apex Court Held, while allowing the Appeal: An FIR will not stand vitiated because a Preliminary Enquiry has not been conducted. Since an Accused public servant does not have a right to be afforded a chance to explain the alleged Disproportionate Assets to the Investigating Officer before the filing of a charge sheet, a similar right cannot be granted to the Accused before the filing of an FIR by making a Preliminary Enquiry mandatory.

The precedents of this Court and the provisions of the CBI Manual make it abundantly clear that a Preliminary Enquiry is not mandatory in all cases which involve allegations of corruption. The decision of the Constitution Bench in LalitaKumari (supra) holds that if the information received discloses the commission of a cognizable offence at the outset, no Preliminary Enquiry would be required. It also clarified that the scope of a Preliminary Enquiry is not to check the veracity of the information received, but only to scrutinize whether it discloses the commission of a cognizable offence. Similarly, para 9.1 of the CBI Manual notes that a Preliminary Enquiry is required only if the information (whether verified or unverified) does not disclose the commission of a cognizable offence. Even when a Preliminary Enquiry is initiated, it has to stop as soon as the officer ascertains that enough material has been collected which discloses the commission of a cognizable offence.

Since the institution of a Preliminary Enquiry in cases of corruption is not made mandatory before the registration of an FIR under the Code of Criminal Procedure, PC Act or even the CBI Manual, for this Court to issue a direction to that affect will be tantamount to stepping into the legislative domain. Hence, in case the information received by the CBI, through a complaint or a "source information" under Chapter 8, discloses the commission of a cognizable offence, it can directly register a Regular Case instead of conducting a Preliminary Enquiry, where the officer is satisfied that the information discloses the commission of a cognizable offence.

Single Judge of the Telangana High Court has acted completely beyond the settled parameters which govern the power to quash an FIR. The Single Judge has donned the role of a Chartered Accountant. The Single Judge has completely ignored that the Court was not at the stage of trial or considering an appeal against a verdict in a trial. The Single Judge has enquired into the material adduced by the Respondents, compared it with the information provided by the CBI in the FIR and their counter-affidavit, and then pronounced a verdict on the merits of each individual allegation raised by the Respondents largely relying upon the documents filed by them (by considering them to be 'known sources of income' within the meaning of Section 13(1)(e) of the PC Act). This exercised has been justified on account of the Appellant not having conducted a Preliminary Enquiry and hence, not having addressed the Respondents' objections relying upon the documents adduced by them. The reasons provided by the Single Judge for entering the merits of the dispute while quashing the FIR are specious. While exercising its jurisdiction Under Article 226 of the Constitution to adjudicate on a petition seeking the quashing of an FIR, the High Court should have only considered whether the contents of the FIR-as they stand and, on their face, -prima facie make out a cognizable offence.

In the present case, the Appellant is challenging the very "source" of the

Respondents' income and the questioning the assets acquired by them based on such income. Hence, at the stage of quashing of an FIR where the Court only has to ascertain whether the FIR prima facie makes out the commission of a cognizable offence, reliance on the documents produced by the Respondents to quash the FIR would be contrary to fundamental principles of law. The High Court has gone far beyond the ambit of its jurisdiction by virtually conducting a trial in an effort to absolve the Respondents.

At this stage, FIR cannot be quashed.

Therefore, impugned judgment set aside.

CHAPTER THIRTEEN

Rajesh Gupta Vs. State through Central Bureau of Investigation, 2022

Hon'ble Judges/Coram: Vineet Saran and J.K. Maheshwari, JJ.

Act/ Sections: Code of Criminal Procedure, 1973 (CrPC) - Section 161; Prevention Of Corruption Act, 1988 - Section 7, Prevention Of Corruption Act, 1988 - Section 13(1), Prevention Of Corruption Act, 1988 - Section 13(2), Prevention Of Corruption Act, 1988 - Section 20

No. of pages of the Original Judgement: 08

Citation: MANU/SC/0527/2022

Case Note: Criminal - Conviction - Legality - Sections 7 & 13(2) read with Section 13(1)(d) of the Prevention of Corruption Act, 1988 ("PC Act") - Present appeal has been filed questioning the validity of the judgment passed by the High Court confirming the judgment passed by Special Judge, convicting the Appellant for the offences under Sections 7 & 13(2) read with Section 13(1)(d) of the PC Act and the order of sentence - Whether impugned order of conviction is liable to be set aside?

Facts: The Appellant is an Accused in a corruption case under the PC Act. As per prosecution allegations, the Appellant, who was the Assistant Commissioner of Income Tax, Circle 20(1) at the concerned point of time demanded and accepted the bribe of Rs. 15,000 from the complainant PW-3 Madhu Bala in regard to scrutiny of her case, which was pending with the Appellant. The Trial Court, vide judgment concluded that the Appellant, while working as public servant (Assistant Commissioner of Income Tax, Circle 20(1)), demanded bribe from the complainant PW3-Madhu Bala and in pursuance of his demand, accepted bribe/illegal gratification of Rs.

15,000 from her on 9.3.2000 in his office (cabin/chamber). Thus by corrupt and illegal means, he abused his position as a public servant and obtained pecuniary advantage for himself. The Appellant was found guilty for the charge under Sections 7 & 13(2) read with Section 13(1)(d) of PC Act. The High Court relying upon the testimony of PW3-Madhu Bala, who was able to identify the conversation Exb. P2 (cassette) from the transcript though found inaudible and without proof of non-tampering the same, concluded that the demand was proved. On the point of acceptance, relying upon the version of PW3 Madhu Bala, who was said to put Rs. 15,000 in a note sheet towards visitor's side of the table underneath a dak-pad and in reference to the CFSL report, proved the acceptance of bribe demanded by the Appellant. In addition, drawing presumption under Section 20 of PC Act, confirmed the findings of the Trial Court and the sentence so awarded. Aggrieved by the said judgments, this appeal has been filed.

Hon'ble Apex Court Held, while allowing the appeal: 1. Except for the testimony of PW3 Madhu Bala (complainant), there is no corroborative evidence of demand, either on 7.3.2000 or 9.3.2000. The law is well-settled by the judgments of this Court in Panna Damodar Rathi v. State of Maharashtra and Ayyasami v. State of Tamil Nadu, whereby it has been clarified that the sole testimony of the complainant, who is the interested witness, cannot be relied upon without having corroboration with the independent evidence.

2. For an offence Under Section 7 of PC Act, the demand of illegal gratification is a sine qua non to prove the guilt. Mere recovery of currency notes cannot constitute an offence Under Section 7 of PC Act, unless it is proved beyond reasonable doubt that Accused voluntarily accepted the money, knowing it to be a bribe. The proof of acceptance of illegal gratification can follow only if there is proof of demand.

3. There is no iota of evidence by which the demand can be proved. Thus, the conclusion of the Trial Court and the High Court to prove the demand is based on surmises and erratic approach ignoring the legal position as enunciated, which cannot be sustained on the facts of the case.

4. The concurrent findings recorded by the Trial Court, and affirmed by the High Court, are not based on due appreciation of the material brought on record in the right perspective. In fact, it is a case in which no cogent evidence is available to prove the guilt of the Accused for an offence Under Sections 7 & 13(2) read with Section 13(1)(d) of PC Act. As In the case at

hand, the concurrent findings in the judgments of the Courts below cannot dissuade this Court from interfering in a case like this where the findings of conviction have been recorded merely on conjectures and erratic evaluation of evidence. The Court is always having an obligation of judicial conscience to correct the errors where the same are manifest. The judgments of the Courts below suffer from serious infirmities and manifest error. There is no proof of demand at pre-trap stage or during trap. The Courts must not over-look the fundamental principle of ignorance of Accused till the charge levelled against the Appellant is established beyond reasonable doubt. Therefore, the conviction of the Appellant has not been proved and the evaluation is based on conjectures and erratic evaluation.

5. The concurrent judgments of the Trial Court as well as of the High Court are set aside and the Appellant is to be held not guilty of the charges against him. Appeal allowed.

CHAPTER FOURTEEN

K. Shanthamma Vs. The State of Telangana, 2022

Hon'ble Judges/Coram: Ajay Rastogi and Abhay Shreeniwas Oka, JJ.

Act/ Sections: Code of Criminal Procedure, 1973 (CrPC) - Section 161, Code of Criminal Procedure, 1973 (CrPC) - Section 164, Code of Criminal Procedure, 1973 (CrPC) - Section 313; Constitution of India - Article 136; Prevention of Corruption Act, 1988 - Section 7, Prevention Of Corruption Act, 1988 - Section 13, Prevention Of Corruption Act, 1988 - Section 13(1), Prevention Of Corruption Act, 1988 - Section 13(2), Prevention Of Corruption Act, 1988 - Section 20

No. of pages of the Original Judgement: 06

Citation: AIR2022SC1134, (2022)4SCC574, MANU/SC/0218/2022

Case Note: Criminal - Conviction - Validity - Sections 7 and 13(1)(d) of Prevention of Corruption Act, 1988 ('the PC Act') - Appeal in present case is against impugned judgment of conviction under Sections 7 and 13(1)(d) read with Section 13(2) of the PC Act - Whether conviction of the Appellant for the offences punishable under Sections 7 and 13(1)(d) read with Section 13(2) of the PC Act is sustainable?

Facts: The Special Court under the Prevention of Corruption Act, 1988 (for short 'the PC Act') convicted the Appellant for the offences punishable under Sections 7 and 13(1)(d) read with Section 13(2) of the PC Act. The order of conviction has been confirmed in appeal by the High Court of Telangana. Appellant submitted that the demand for a bribe by the Appellant was not proved, and the evidence of PW1 to that effect is an improvement.

Hon'ble Apex Court Held, while allowing the appeal: 1. The offence under Section 7 of the PC Act relating to public servants taking bribe requires a demand of illegal gratification and the acceptance thereof. The proof of demand of bribe by a public servant and its acceptance by him is sine quo non for establishing the offence Under Section 7 of the PC Act.

2. Thus, the version of PW1 in his examination-in-chief about the demand made by the Appellant from time to time is an improvement. LW8 did not enter the Appellant's chamber at the time of trap. There is no other evidence of the alleged demand. Thus, the evidence of PW1 about the demand for bribe by the Appellant is not at all reliable. Hence, we conclude that the demand made by the Appellant has not been conclusively proved.

3. Thus, this is a case where the demand of illegal gratification by the Appellant was not proved by the prosecution. Thus, the demand which is sine quo non for establishing the offence under Section 7 was not established.

4. Hence, the impugned Judgments will have to be set aside. The conviction of the Appellant for the offences punishable under Sections 7 and 13(1)(d) read with Section 13(2) of the PC Act is set aside and the Appellant is acquitted of the charges framed against her. Appeal allowed.

CHAPTER FIFTEEN

J. Sekar Vs. Directorate of Enforcement, 2022

Hon'ble Judges/Coram: Vineet Saran and J.K. Maheshwari, JJ.

Act/ Sections: Code of Criminal Procedure, 1973 (CrPC) - Section 161, Code of Criminal Procedure, 1973 (CrPC) - Section 173(2), Code of Criminal Procedure, 1973 (CrPC) - Section 300, Code of Criminal Procedure, 1973 (CrPC) - Section 482; Constitution of India - Article 20(2); Indian Penal Code, 1860 (IPC) - Section 120B, Indian Penal Code, 1860 (IPC) - Section 409, Indian Penal Code, 1860 (IPC) - Section 420; Prevention Of Corruption Act, 1988 - Section 13(1), Prevention Of Corruption Act, 1988 - Section 13(2); Prevention Of Money-laundering Act, 2002 - Section 2(1), Prevention Of Money-laundering Act, 2002 - Section 3, Prevention Of Money-laundering Act, 2002 - Section 4, Prevention Of Money-laundering Act, 2002 - Section 5(1), Prevention Of Money-laundering Act, 2002 - Section 5(5), Prevention Of Money-laundering Act, 2002 - Section 8(1), Prevention Of Money-laundering Act, 2002 - Section 8(5), Prevention Of Money-laundering Act, 2002 - Section 44(1)

No. of pages of the Original Judgement:

Citation: MANU/SC/0596/2022

Case Note: Criminal - Quashing of proceedings - Section 120-B read with Section 409, 420 of Indian Penal Code, 1860 (IPC) - Section 13(2), read with Section 13(1)(c) and 13(1)(d) of the Prevention of Corruption Act, 1988 (PC Act) - Section 482 of the Code of Criminal Procedure, 1973 (CrPC) - Sections 3 and 4 of the Prevention of Money Laundering Act, 2002 (PMLA) - High Court vide impugned judgment rejected the petition seeking quashing of proceedings - Hence the present appeal - Whether impugned judgment in view of the facts and circumstances of the case sustainable or liable to be set aside?

Facts: The present appeal was filed against the impugned judgment dismissing the petition filed for quashing of proceedings. The impugned judgment rejected Appellant's contention that FIR with respect to Schedule offence was closed for want of evidence and in absence of connected evidence with a crime of Schedule offence, prosecution for offences under Sections 3 & 4 of the PMLA unsustainable. It was also held that the offence of money laundering is independent of the Schedule offence because PMLA deals with the process or activity with respect to the proceeds of crime including concealment, possession, acquisition or use. However, in the light of the explanation of Section 44(1) of PMLA, the argument of the Appellant was repelled. Appellant, Managing Partner of a partnership firm engaged in sand mining was subjected to case registered by CBI for offences under Sections 120-B r/w 409, 420 of IPC and Section 13(2), r/w 13(1)(c) and 13(1)(d) of the PC Act against the Appellant and two others.

For proceeds of crime, as defined under Section 2(1)(u) of PMLA, the property seized would be relevant and its possession with recovery and claim thereto must be innocent. In the present case, the Schedule offence has not been made out because of lack of evidence. The Adjudicating Authority, at the time of refusing to continue the order of attachment under PMLA, was of the opinion that the record regarding banks and its officials who may be involved, is not on record. Therefore, for lack of identity of the source of collected money, it could not be reasonably believed by the Deputy Director (ED) that the unaccounted money is connected with the commission of offence under PMLA. Even in cases of PMLA, the Court cannot proceed on the basis of preponderance of probabilities. On perusal of the statement of Objects and Reasons specified in PMLA, it is the stringent law brought by Parliament to check money laundering. Thus, the allegation must be proved beyond reasonable doubt in the Court. Even otherwise, it is incumbent upon the Court to look into the allegation and the material collected in support thereto and to find out whether the prima facie offence is made out. Unless the allegations are substantiated by the authorities and proved against a person in the court of law, the person is innocent.

Looking to the facts as discussed hereinabove and the ratio of the judgments of this Court in Radheshyam Kejriwal (supra) and Ashoo Surendranath Tewari (supra), the chance to prove the allegations even for the purpose of provisions of PMLA in the Court are bleak. Therefore, till the allegations are proved, the Appellant would be innocent. The High Court by the impugned order has recorded the finding without due consideration of the letter of the I.T. Department and other material in right perspective. Therefore, these findings of the High Court cannot be sustained.

Accordingly, appeal is allowed.

CHAPTER SIXTEEN

The State by S.P. through the Spe. CBI Vs. Uttamchand Bohra, 2021

Hon'ble Judges/Coram: K.M. Joseph and S. Ravindra Bhat, JJ.

Act/ Sections: Code of Criminal Procedure, 1973 (CrPC) - Section 161, Code of Criminal Procedure, 1973 (CrPC) - Section 173, Code of Criminal Procedure, 1973 (CrPC) - Section 209, Code of Criminal Procedure, 1973 (CrPC) - Section 226, Code of Criminal Procedure, 1973 (CrPC) - Section 227, Code of Criminal Procedure, 1973 (CrPC) - Section 228, Code of Criminal Procedure, 1973 (CrPC) - Section 239, Code of Criminal Procedure, 1973 (CrPC) - Section 397, Code of Criminal Procedure, 1973 (CrPC) - Section 401; Indian Penal Code, 1860 (IPC) - Section 107, Indian Penal Code, 1860 (IPC) - Section 109, Indian Penal Code, 1860 (IPC) - Section 120A, Indian Penal Code, 1860 (IPC) - Section 120B; Prevention Of Corruption Act, 1988 - Section 7, Prevention Of Corruption Act, 1988 - Section 13(1), Prevention Of Corruption Act, 1988 - Section 13(2)

No. of pages of the Original Judgement: 12

Citation: MANU/SC/1214/2021

Case Note: Criminal - Quashing - Complaint alleging abatement of conspiracy with public servant -Sections 109, 120B of the Indian Penal Code, 1860 (IPC) and Section 13(2) read with Section 13(1)(e) of the Prevention of Corruption Act, 1988 (PCA) - Accused alleged of amassing wealth disproportionate to income -High Court quashed chargesheet filed holding mere in possession of document could not incriminate him - Hence, the present appeal - Whether High Court erred in quashing the charge sheet in question?

Facts: High Court vide impugned judgment quashed charge sheet against the Respondent (Accused No. 5 before the Trial Court). Trial court had earlier rejected application under Section 239 of the Code of Criminal Procedure seeking his discharge. Accused was alleged of abetting and/or conspiring with the principal Accused, a public servant (A-1), so as to permit him to accumulate assets disproportionate to his known sources of income. Hence, the present appeal by State.

Hon'ble Apex Court Held, while dismissing the Appeal: The factual narration in this case would reveal that the Respondent, was not a public officer or public servant. He cannot therefore, be charged with committing an offence Under Section 13(1)(e) read with Section 13(2) of the PCA. There is no allegation that he received any monetary or other benefit, or that he held the property in his name for the benefit of A-1.

The chargesheet further does not contain any allegation which can amount to an offence under Section 109 Indian Penal Code. The prosecution has not suggested that he abetted A-1 to acquire disproportionate assets in any manner; the only allegation is that the title deeds to the flat, which is in the name of M/s. Raviteja Trading Co. Pvt. Ltd. was seized from his custody and that he had instructed his employee to witness the document. An allegation of the existence of signatures of as a witness to the sale deed cannot amount to his aiding or abetting A-1 to acquire disproportionate assets. Witnessing a sale deed is a formal requirement. Likewise, the fact that the sale deed was in his residence cannot satisfy the ingredient of any of the offences alleged against him.

The FIR in the present case names only A-1 and A-2 as the Accused. The sale deed had already been seized from Respondent's house by then.

The present appeal lacks merit. It is therefore dismissed.

CHAPTER SEVENTEEN

Banka Sneha Sheela Vs. The State of Telangana and Ors., 2021

Hon'ble Judges/Coram: Rohinton Fali Nariman and Hrishikesh Roy, JJ.

Citation: AIR2021SC3656, (2021)9SCC415, MANU/SC/0493/2021

Case Note: Criminal - Preventive Detention - Complaints of fraud and cheating - Challenge against order directing detention dismissed - Section 3(2) of the Telangana Prevention of Dangerous Activities of Bootleggers, Dacoits, Drug-Offenders, Goondas, Immoral Traffic Offenders Land-Grabbers, Spurious Seed Offenders, Insecticide Offenders, Fertiliser Offenders, Food Adulteration Offenders, Fake Document Offenders, Scheduled Commodities Offenders, Forest Offenders, Gaming Offenders, Sexual Offenders, Explosive Substances Offenders, Arms Offenders, Cyber Crime Offenders and White Collar or Financial Offenders Act, 1986 (Act) - Whether dismissal of petition challenging detention order justified?

No. of pages of the Original Judgement: 15

Facts: The present appeal was filed against the order dismissing Petitioner's writ petition filed to challenge Preventive Detention Order passed against her husband. The detention order referred five FIRs filed against the Detenu under Sections 420, 406 and 506 of the Indian Penal Code, 1860. Acts alleged caused loss of faith and trust among investors in stock trading fearing similar cheating. The activities alleged to also cause to be disturbance in the public.

Hon'ble Apex Court Held, while allowing the Appeals: For 'public order' to be disturbed, there must in turn be public disorder. Mere contravention of law such as indulging in cheating or criminal breach of trust certainly affects 'law and order' but before it can be said to affect 'public order', it must affect the community or the public at large.

There can be no doubt that what is alleged in the five FIRs pertain to the realm of 'law and order' in that various acts of cheating are ascribed to the Detenu which are punishable under the three Sections of the Indian Penal Code set out in the five FIRs. A close reading of the Detention Order would make it clear that the reason for the said Order is not any apprehension of widespread public harm, danger or alarm but is only because the Detenu was successful in obtaining anticipatory bail/bail from the Courts in each of the five FIRs. If a person is granted anticipatory bail/bail wrongly, there are well-known remedies in the ordinary law to take care of the situation. The State can always appeal against the bail order granted and/or apply for cancellation of bail. The mere successful obtaining of anticipatory bail/bail orders being the real ground for detaining the Detenu, there can be no doubt that the harm, danger or alarm or feeling of security among the general public spoken of in Section 2(a) of the Telangana Prevention of Dangerous Activities Act is make believe and totally absent in the facts of the present case.

On the facts of this case, a possible apprehension of breach of law and order can be said to be made out if it is apprehended that the Detenu, if set free, will continue to cheat gullible persons. This may be a good ground to appeal against the bail orders granted and/or to cancel bail but certainly cannot provide the springboard to move under a preventive detention statute. Detention order quashed on this ground. The impugned judgment is set aside and the Detenu is ordered to be freed forthwith. Accordingly, the appeal is allowed.

CHAPTER EIGHTEEN

Khaja Bilal Ahmed Vs. State of Telangana and Ors., 2019

Hon'ble Judges/Coram: Dr. D.Y. Chandrachud and Hrishikesh Roy, JJ.

Act/ Sections: Cyber Crime Offenders and White Collar or Financial Offenders Act 1986 - Section 13; Code of Criminal Procedure, 1973 (CrPC) - Section 167, Code of Criminal Procedure, 1973 (CrPC) - Section 167(2); Constitution of India - Article 136; Criminal Law Amendment Act, 1932 - Section 7; Indian Arms Act, 1878 - Section 27; Indian Penal Code, 1860 (IPC) - Section 34, Indian Penal Code, 1860 (IPC) - Section 120B, Indian Penal Code, 1860 (IPC) - Section 147, Indian Penal Code, 1860 (IPC) - Section 148, Indian Penal Code, 1860 (IPC) - Section 149, Indian Penal Code, 1860 (IPC) - Section 153, Indian Penal Code, 1860 (IPC) - Section 153(A), Indian Penal Code, 1860 (IPC) - Section 159, Indian Penal Code, 1860 (IPC) - Section 188, Indian Penal Code, 1860 (IPC) - Section 302, Indian Penal Code, 1860 (IPC) - Section 307, Indian Penal Code, 1860 (IPC) - Section 323, Indian Penal Code, 1860 (IPC) - Section 324, Indian Penal Code, 1860 (IPC) - Section 332, Indian Penal Code, 1860 (IPC) - Section 341, Indian Penal Code, 1860 (IPC) - Section 353, Indian Penal Code, 1860 (IPC) - Section 364, Indian Penal Code, 1860 (IPC) - Section 374, Indian Penal Code, 1860 (IPC) - Section 382, Indian Penal Code, 1860 (IPC) - Section 427, Indian Penal Code, 1860 (IPC) - Section 447, Indian Penal Code, 1860 (IPC) - Section 448, Indian Penal Code, 1860 (IPC) - Section 506; Prevention Of Damage To Public Property Act, 1984 - Section 4; West Bengal (Prevention of Violent Activities) Act, 1970 - Section 10, West Bengal (Prevention of Violent Activities) Act, 1970 - Section 11, West Bengal (Prevention of Violent Activities) Act, 1970 - Section 12, West Bengal (Prevention of Violent Activities) Act, 1970 - Section 12(1).

No. of pages of the Original Judgement: 11

Citation: (2020)13SCC632, MANU/SC/1781/2019

Case Note: Criminal - Detention order - Quashing of - Appellant was detained on premise that dangerous activities of offender and his associates were stated to have caused panic and feeling of insecurity in minds of general public - Brother of Appellant filed writ petition challenging order of detention - High Court dismissed Writ Petition challenging order of detention - Hence, present appeal - Whether detention order liable to be set aside.

Facts: The Appellant was detained under the provisions of Sub-section 2 of Section 3 of the Telangana Offenders Act 1986. The order of detention thereafter proceeds to state that the Appellant was implicated in Crime which was under investigation. The dangerous activities of the offender and his associates were stated to have caused panic and a feeling of insecurity in the minds of the general public. The brother of the Appellant filed a Writ Petition challenging the order of detention. On appeal, the High Court dismissed the Writ Petition challenging the order of detention.

Hon'ble Apex Court Held, while allowing the appeal: (i) The detention order had to be set aside on the grounds that reference to stale and irrelevant grounds in the detention order by the detaining authority and the manner in which the order of confirmation was presented before this Court, casts doubt on the existence of the order of confirmation in the first place. As regards the registration of Crime, the Appellant was released on bail consequent upon the failure of the investigating authority to file a charge-sheet within ninety days. A charge-sheet, had not been filed till date. There was no reasonable basis on which the detaining authority could have come to a conclusion that on being released on bail, the Appellant would in all probability indulge in prejudicial activity and it was necessary to detain him, to prevent him from engaging in prejudicial activity.

CHAPTER NINETEEN

Chhattisgarh State Industrial Development Corporation Ltd. and Ors. Vs. Amar Infrastructure Ltd. and Ors., 2017

Hon'ble Judges/Coram: Arun Mishra and Amitava Roy, JJ.

No. of pages of the Original Judgement: 11

Citation: (2017)5SCC387, MANU/SC/0296/2017

Case Note: Commercial - Rejections of tender - Necessary qualification - High Court quashed contract given to Appellant bidder by Appellant Corporation - Hence, present appeal - Whether having Hot Mix Plant was necessary qualification.

Facts: Tender was floated by the Chhattisgarh State Industrial Development Corporation Ltd. (CSIDC). Tender was floated by the CSIDC for the work within the stipulated time period of 18 months and tenders were invited online. The online bids were submitted. The CSIDC opened the tenders for determining whether the bidders satisfied the pre-qualification criteria. Based upon the information supplied by the bidders, the CSIDC prepared charts of technical evaluation documents. The documents of technical evaluation filed by CSIDC were signed by the Executive Engineer and the document filed by the Respondent No. 1 did not bear signatures of any official. Two bidders including the Appellant bidder were found qualified. It was opined by the Evaluation Committee that they fulfilled all the requisite qualifications. The bid submitted by the Appellant bidder was ranked as L-1 as compared to that of another bidder whose bid was ranked as L-2. Ultimately the bid L-1 of the Appellant bidder had been accepted and work order had been issued by the CSIDC to it.

The Respondent was disqualified on the ground that its construction experience was not found as per the requisite criteria indicated in experience certificate, quantity of DLC (M-10) i.e., 3194 cum submitted under the key activities of construction experience of requisite quantity of work done was not in accordance with the nomenclature of PWD SOR. In the nomenclature of DLC in SOR there was no M-20 type of concrete, as such the amount of DLC as presented in the certificate had been rejected. The petition filed before the High Court by one of the unsuccessful bidders was dismissed. However, the Respondent filed a representation not against the successful bidder but against second bidder to the effect that it had been found eligible for opening financial bid despite not having a Hot Mix-Plant. The High Court directed the Superintendent of Police to depute an independent and competent officer from the Cyber Crime Cell of the State Police to inspect, examine and analyse the data available on the computer of the CSIDC. The report was filed and the High Court found that the document which were placed on record; one filed by the CSIDC and other filed by the Appellant were substantially different with respect to the fact whether Hot Mix Plant was owned by the second bidder and also that modification had been made in the document. Thus, the High Court had opined that L-2 tenderer basically was not qualified to participate and had been made to qualify for opening of its financial bid in order to give the contract anyhow or somehow to the Appellant bidder. It concluded that second bidder was illegally included in the qualified list of bidders by the Technical Evaluation Committee. Thus, the contract granted to the Appellant bidder was quashed and at the same time further police investigation had been ordered so as to fix the responsibility for the manipulations made in the document filed by the CSIDC and/or by the Respondent.

Hon'ble Apex Court Held That: (i) In the list of mandatory plant etc. necessary for pre-qualification criteria, the Hot Mix Plant was not mentioned. Thus, it was not a pre-requisite to qualify for opening financial bid. In the list of minimum plant, equipment's and shuttering provided in Clause 51 of the contract document, 18 items were mentioned in which again the Hot Mix Plant was not mentioned in the list of "Minimum plant equipment and Shuttering".

(ii) In case, any of the minimum equipment is not available and certificate is not appended to the bid, the financial bid was not to be opened. Both the bidders L-1 and L-2 were technically qualified for opening of their financial bids. The opinion expressed by the High Court that L-2 was made to be qualified in spite of the fact that it was not having Hot Mix Plant, thus, could not be accepted as available ground to disqualify L-2 tenderer.

(iii) There was no manipulation in the mandatory requirements and may be that P-4 was prepared but that was of no consequence as deficiency of Hot Mix Plant, even if placed before Committee, would not have tilted the balance in favour of the Respondent. The Committee on that basis could not have disqualified the L-2 tenderer. There was no merit in the petition filed by the Respondent in the High Court. Thus, the impugned judgment, order and directions passed by the High Court were set aside.

CHAPTER TWENTY

State Vs. M. Murugesan and Ors., 2020

Hon'ble Judges/Coram: L. Nageswara Rao and Hemant Gupta, JJ.

Act/ Sections: Code of Criminal Procedure, 1973 (CrPC) - Section 97, Code of Criminal Procedure, 1973 (CrPC) - Section 200, Code of Criminal Procedure, 1973 (CrPC) - Section 439, Code of Criminal Procedure, 1973 (CrPC) - Section 482; Constitution of India - Article 32, Constitution of India - Article 226

No. of pages of the Original Judgement: 07

Citation: AIR2020SC514, (2020)15SCC251, MANU/SC/0034/2020

Case Note: Criminal - Heterogeneous Committee - Constitution of - Validity - Section 439 of Code of Criminal Procedure, 1973 (CrPC) - State was aggrieved against an order passed by High Court constituting a Heterogeneous Committee of named persons to give its recommendations on reforms that, could be brought into practice for reformation, rehabilitation and re-integration of Convict/Accused person to society and best practices for improving quality of investigation.

Facts: State is aggrieved against an order passed by the High Court constituting a Heterogeneous Committee of named persons to give its recommendations on the reforms that can be brought into practice for reformation, rehabilitation and re-integration of the Convict/Accused person to society and best practices for improving the quality of investigation. The Committee was mandated to submit report within eight weeks and that the State was directed to furnish data for each District. The Committee was to scrutinize the same and submit the final data separately along with the report. The State was directed to provide office room for the Committee to conduct its meetings and to keep the documents and other materials in safe custody. Such directions came to be passed in a matter pertaining to grant of bail under Section 439 of the Code of Criminal Procedure, 1973. The High Court had admitted the Accused to bail on 18th February, 2019 subject to certain conditions but passed an order to call for the details of the cases registered by the Police, final report filed, trial conducted and the result of such cases. The details were to bring to light the manner in which the entire criminal justice system is operating in the State. In pursuance of the directions so issued and the data provided, the impugned order was passed by the learned Single Bench.

Hon'ble Apex Court Held, while allowing the appeal: 1. The Hon'ble Single Bench has committed grave illegality in retaining the file after grant of bail to the Accused on 18th February, 2019. The jurisdiction of the High Court came to an end, when an application for grant of bail under Section 439 of the CrPC was finally decided.

2. This Court in Davinder Pal Singh Bhullar referred to a case reported as Simrikhia v. Dolley Mukherjee and Chhabi Mukherjee and Anr wherein the Court observed that inherent powers under Section 482 of the CrPC cannot be exercised to do something which is expressly barred under the Code. It was held that inherent powers cannot be exercised assuming that the statute conferred an unfettered and arbitrary jurisdiction, nor can the High Court act at its whim or caprice. The Code does not confer unlimited/ unfettered jurisdiction on the High Court as the "ends of justice" and "abuse of the process of the court" have to be dealt with in accordance with law and not otherwise. The High Court has not been given nor does it possess any inherent power to make any order, which in the opinion of the court, could be in the interest of justice as the statutory provision is not intended to bypass the procedure prescribed. It was also held that the High Court can always issue appropriate direction in exercise of its power under Article 226 of the Constitution of India at the behest of an aggrieved person, if the court is convinced that the power of investigation has been exercised by an investigating officer mala fide or the matter is not investigated at all, but even in such a case, the High Court cannot direct the police as to how the investigation is to be conducted but can insist only for the observance of due process as provided in the Code.

3. This Court in a judgment reported as Sangitaben Shaileshbhai Datanta v. State of Gujarat was examining a question where a court after grant of bail to an Accused ordered the Accused and their relatives to undergo scientific test viz. lie detector, brain mapping and Narco-Analysis. This Court held that direction of the court to carry out such tests is not only in

contravention to the first principles of criminal law jurisprudence but also violates statutory requirements.

4. In another judgment reported as Reserve Bank of India v. General Manager, Cooperative Bank Deposit A/C HR. Sha and Ors, Reserve Bank of India challenged an order passed on an application under Section 439 of the CrPC, wherein an argument was raised that the poor depositors are not paid by the Bank out of the amount which has been received by the Bank. The Court issued directions that the Bank should start distributing the amount which is so far recovered by them from the Accused. The Bank was directed to furnish details of the money paid to the poor depositors. The Accused as well as the Investigating Officer and the Administrator of the Bank were directed to remain present in the Court. This Court found that such directions are beyond the scope of an application for bail filed by the Accused under Section 439 of the CrPC.

5. Learned Single Judge has collated data from the State and made it part of the order after the decision of the bail application as if the Court had the inherent jurisdiction to pass any order under the guise of improving the criminal justice system in the State. The jurisdiction of the Court under Section 439 of the CrPC is limited to grant or not to grant bail pending trial. Even though the object of the Hon'ble Judge was laudable but the jurisdiction exercised was clearly erroneous. The effort made by the Hon'ble Judge may be academically proper to be presented at an appropriate forum but such directions could not be issued under the colour of office of the Court.

6. The order passed by the High Court is not sustainable in law and the same is set aside. Consequently, the appeal is allowed.

CHAPTER TWENTY-ONE

Rini Johar and Ors. Vs. State of M.P. and Ors., 2016

Hon'ble Judges/Coram: Dipak Misra and S.K. Singh, JJ.

Citation: AIR2016SC2679, (2016)11SCC703, MANU/SC/0667/2016

Case Note: Criminal - Arrest and Detention - Legality thereof - Entitlement to compensation - Section 66D of Information Technology Act, 2000 (Act); Sections 420 and 34 of Indian Penal Code, 1860 (IPC); Sections 41 and 41A of Code of Criminal Procedure, 1973 (CrPC); Article 21 of Constitution of India, 1950 - Petitioners were challenging validity and legality of their arrest pursuant to complaint filed by Informant, Respondent No. 8 - Whether provisions enshrined under Section 41A to 41C of CrPC, had been violated in process of arresting of Petitioners - Whether Petitioners would be entitled to any compensation on bedrock of public law remedy- Magistrate rejected prayer to discharge accused persons in respect of Section 66A(b) of Act, read with Section 420 and 34 of IPC- Whether continuance of criminal proceedings would be justified?

Facts: Informant, Respondent No. 8, had sent an email to company for purchase of machine Aura Cam, 6000, which was an Aura Imaging Equipment, in India and concerned company sent an email to Respondent making a reference to Petitioner No. 1. Informant visited Petitioner No. 1 at Pune and being satisfied decided to purchase a lesser price machine i.e. "Twinaura Pro" and paid a sum of Rs. 2,50,000/- for which a hand written receipt was given as proof of payment. During the course of said meeting, 8th Respondent expressed his desire to purchase a laptop of Progen of which Petitioner No. 1 was representative. In pursuance of discussion, laptop was given to him who acknowledged it by stating that he owed a sum of Rs. 4,800/- as balance consideration towards Aura Cam and an amount of USD 350 towards laptop. An assurance was given for remitting money within a short time. Respondent No. 8 had never raised any grievance relating either to machine or laptop. Respondent No. 8 filed a complaint before Inspector General of Police, alleging that Petitioner No. 1 and Mr. Guy Coggin had committed fraud of US 10,500. On basis of complaint made, FIR No. 24/2012 under Section 420 and 34 of IPC and Section 66D of Act, was registered against the Petitioners by Cyber Police Headquarters. Petitioners were arrested from their residence at Pune. After they were arrested, they were taken from Pune to Bhopal in an un-reserved railway compartment marked-'viklang' (handicapped). Despite request, Petitioner No. 2, an old lady, was not taken to a doctor, and was compelled to lie on cold floor of train compartment without any food and water. Indignified treatment and humiliation faced by Petitioners had been mentioned in great detail. They were produced before Magistrate at Bhopal and Petitioner No. 2 was enlarged on bail after being in custody for about 17 days and Petitioner No. 1 was released after more than three weeks. Petitioners alleged that they were forced to pay Rs. 5 lakhs to Respondent No. 3, Dy. S.P. Cyber Cell, Bhopal. Director General of Police had appointed Inspector General of Police, CID to enquire into allegations as regards violation of provisions enshrined under Section 41A to 41C of CrPC. In pursuance of order passed by Director General, an enquiry had been conducted by Inspector General of Police Administration, CID, Bhopal. It had been styled as "preliminary enquiry". Magistrate passed an order discharging Petitioners in respect of offence punishable under Section 66D of Act. However, Magistrate had opined that there was prima facie case for offence punishable under Section 66A(b) of Act, read with Section 420 and 34 of IPC.

Hon'ble Apex Court Held, while disposing off the petitions: 1. Court in Arnesh Kumar v. State of Bihar and Anr., while dwelling upon concept of arrest, was compelled to observe that Arrest brings humiliation, curtails freedom and casts scars forever.

2. In said authority, it has been held that Section 41A of CrPC, made it clear that where arrest of a person is not required under Section 41(1) of CrPC, police officer is required to issue notice directing accused to appear before him at a specified place and time. Law obliged such an accused to appear before police officer and it further mandated that, if such an accused complied with terms of notice, he would not be arrested, unless for reasons to be recorded, police officer was of opinion that arrest was necessary. At this stage also, condition precedent for arrest as envisaged under Section 41 of CrPC, has to be complied and would be subject to same scrutiny by

Magistrate.

3. On a scrutiny of enquiry report, it was vivid that the arrest of Petitioners was not made by following the procedure of arrest. Section 41A of CrPC, as had been interpreted by this Court had not been followed. Report clearly showed that, there had been number of violations in arrest, and seizure. Circumstances in no case justified manner in which Petitioners were treated.

4. Dignity of Petitioners, a doctor and a practicing Advocate had been seriously jeopardized. Liberty of Petitioner was curtailed in violation of law. Freedom of an individual had its sanctity. When individual liberty was curtailed in an unlawful manner, then victim was likely to feel more anguished, agonized, shaken, perturbed, disillusioned and emotionally torn. It was an assault on his/her identity. Said identity was sacrosanct under Constitution. Therefore, for curtailment of liberty, requisite norms were to be followed. Two ladies had been arrested without following procedure and put in compartment of a train without being produced before local Magistrate from Pune to Bhopal.

5. In present case, there had been violation of Article 21 of Constitution, and Petitioners were compelled to face humiliation. They had been treated with an attitude of insensibility. Not only there were violation of guidelines issued in case of D.K. Basu, there were also flagrant violation of mandate of law enshrined under Section 41 and Section 41A of CrPC. In such a situation, public law remedy which had been postulated in Nilawati Behra, Sube Singh v. State of Haryana, Hardeep Singh v. State of M.P., came into play. Constitutional courts taking note of suffering and humiliation were entitled to grant compensation. In present case, in the facts and circumstances of case, Petitioners were entitled to compensation.

6. Section 66A of Act, had been struck down in its entirety being violative of Article 19(1)(a) of Constitution and not saved under Article 19(2) of Constitution, in Shreya Singhal v. Union of India. Only offence, therefore, that remained was Section 420 of IPC. Magistrate had recorded a finding that, there had been no impersonation. However, he had opined that there were some materials to show that Petitioners had intention to cheat. On a perusal of FIR, it was clear that dispute was purely of a civil nature, but a maladroit effort had been made to give it a criminal colour.

7. In present case, no ingredient of Section 420 of IPC, was remotely attracted. Even if it was a wrong, complainant had to take recourse to civil

action. Present case did not fall in categories where cognizance of offence could be taken by Court and accused could be asked to face trial. Entire case projected a civil dispute and nothing else. Therefore, invoking principle laid down in State of Haryana v. Bhajan Lal, proceedings initiated at instance of 8th Respondent was quashed and the order negativing prayer for discharge of Accused persons was set aside. Prosecution initiated against Petitioners was quashed. Petition allowed.

Adv. Jayprakash Somani's Videos On Law

1) SLP in Supreme Court / Special Leave Petitions in the Supreme Court of India

2) Transfer of Civil & Criminal Cases by the Supreme Court of India / Transfer of Matrimonial Cases

3) Appellate Jurisdiction of the Supreme Court of India

4) Jurisdictions of the Supreme Court of India

5) Public Interest Litigation in the Supreme Court of India / PIL in Supreme Court

6) Article 32 Writ Petitions in the Supreme Court of India

7) Bail Matters Top 10 Supreme Court Cases

8) FIR Quashing in High Court & Supreme Court

9) Bail & Anticipatory Bail Matters in Supreme Court

10) Insolvency & Bankruptcy Matters in the Supreme Court

11) Insolvency & Bankruptcy Code 2016 Part 1

12) Insolvency & Bankruptcy Code 2016 Part 2

13) Insolvency & Bankruptcy Code 2016 Part 3

14) Corporate Liquidation Process

15) Supreme Court Rules & Procedures Webinar of 2.5 hour on Zoom

16) RDDBFI Act, 1993 (Introduction)

17) The Indian Contact Act 1872

18) Negotiable Instruments Act (Introduction)

19) How to avoid matrimonial disputes& some more videos

20) SEBI Matters in the Supreme Court

21) Matrimonial Matters: Supreme Court's 20 Case Laws

22) Consumer Matters Supreme Court's 20 Case Laws

23) Service Matters Supreme Court's 20 Case Laws

24) How to Search Lawyer for Your Matter

25) Property Matters Supreme Court's 20 Case Laws

26) Bail Matters: Supreme Court's 20 Case Laws

27) Supreme Court / High Court Vacation Benches

28) 69000 Teacher's Recruitment Matters of UP Government in the Supreme Court

29) Contempt of Court Matters in the Supreme Court

30) Advocate Act's Matters in the Supreme Court

31) Business Law Matters in the Supreme Court

32) Banking Matters in the Supreme Court

33) Labour Law Matters in the Supreme Court

34) Arbitration Matters in the Supreme Court

35) Careers in Law -Zoom Webinar by Adv. Jayprakash Somani

36) Civil Matters in the Supreme Court

37) Consumer Protection Act | Consumer Matters in the Supreme Court

38) Corporate Matters in the Supreme Court

39) Criminal Matters in the Supreme Court

40) Role of Respondent in the Supreme Court of India

41) Motor Vehicle Accident Matters in Supreme Court with case laws

42) Article 131 Original Suits in Supreme Court

43) PIL in Supreme Court/ Public Interest Litigations in the Supreme Court of India'

44) CAB Citizenship Amendment Bill is not Unconstitutional

45) Supreme Court of India Cases & Process – Marathi

46) Legal Services Export / Export of Legal Services

47) Transfer of Matrimonial Cases by the Supreme Court of India

48) Public Interest Litigation PIL

49) The Specific Relief Act (Introduction)

50) Corporate Insolvency Resolution Process CIRP

51) ABMM's Career 5 - Careers in Law

52) Transfer of cases by Supreme Court

53) Writ Petitions in High Court & Supreme Court of India

54) Supreme Court Jurisdictions - Appeals, SLP, Writ Petitions, Transfer, Original, Review, Curative

55) LEGAL INDIA TV Show: Cases Handled in Supreme Court

56) Corporate Liquidation Process

57) Legal Services Export / Export of Legal Services

58) Corporate Laws

59) Election Matters- Supreme Court's 20 Case Laws

60) Companies Act, 2013

62) Competition Act, 2002

63) Banking Matters - Supreme Court's 20 Case Laws

64) Election Matters in the Supreme Court

65) Armed Forces Tribunal Matters in the Supreme Court

66) Compassionate Appointment Service matter

67) Foreign Exchange Management Act FEMA

68) Foreign Trade Policy 2021-26 Proposed

69) Customs Act 1962

70) Narcotic Drugs and Psychotropic Substances Act, 1985 NDPS Act

71) Foreign Trade Development & Regulation Act, 1992

72) How to Search Good Advocate in the Supreme Court of India

73) Sr. Adv Vikas Singh's Interview in Nani Palkhivala Wednesday Law Club

74) Indian Penal Code (I. P. C.)

75) Criminal Procedure Code (Cr. P. C.)

76) Commercial Courts & International Arbitration - by Mr. Jaideep Gupta, Senior Advocate in Nani Palkhivala Wednesday Law Club

77) Sr. Adv Ranji Thomos in Nani Palkhivala Wednesday Law Club

78) Urgent Matters in Supreme Court during vacations

79) 498A Bail Matters in Supreme Court

81) 376 Bail Matters in Supreme Court

82) 302, 304, 307, 308 Bail Matters in Supreme Court

83) 138, 420 Bail Matters in Supreme Court

84) POCSO Act Bail Matters in Supreme Court

85) NDPS Act Bail Matters in Supreme Court

86) What is ED (Enforcement Directorate)?

87) Prevention of Money Laundering Act, 2002 (PMLA Act)

88) Insolvency & Bankruptcy Code- Supreme Court Case Laws. Webinar in Nani Palkhivala Wednesday Law Club

89) What is NCLT & NCLAT?

90) Acquittal from 376- Supreme Court's some case laws in Nani Palkhivala Wednesday Law Club dt 28.7.22

91) Insolvency & Bankruptcy in India

92) Can we file case directly in the Supreme Court?

93) Adv. Anuja Pethia has cleared AOR Exam 2021 with 77% marks - Her interview in Nani Palkhivala Wednesday Law Club

94) Customs Act - Supreme Court Case Laws & Interview of AOR Adv. Anuja Pethia in Nani Palkhivala Law Club.

95) The Uttar Pradesh Public Service Tribunals Act, 1976

96) POCSO Act - Supreme Court Case Laws & Interview of AOR Adv. Shoumendu Mukharji & Adv. Nishant Verma in Nani Palkhivala Law Club.

97) Who Can Trigger CIRP Process Under Insolvency Law of India

98) The Uttar Pradesh Government Servant Discipline and Appeal Rules, 1999

99) CIRP Application Under Sec 7 by FC

100) Information Technology Act 2000

101) Uttar Pradesh Recruitment of Dependants of Government Servants Dying in Harness Rules, 1974

102) Foreign Exchange Management Act 1999 & Supreme Court's Case Laws on FEMA & Leading Case of AOR Exam in Nani Palkhivala Law Club.

103) Arbitration and Conciliation Act 1996 & It's Supreme Court Case Laws in Nani Palkhivala Wednesday Law Club.

104) Narcotic Drugs & Psychotropic Substances Act 1985 (NDPS Act) & It's Supreme Court Case Laws in Nani Palkhivala Wednesday Law Club.

105) Recovery of Debts and Bankruptcy Act 1993

106) Uttar Pradesh Land Revenue Code 2006

107) CIRP Application Under Sec 9 by OC

108) CIRP Application Under Sec 10 by CD

109) Hindu Succession Act, 1956

110) Maharashtra Civil Services Rules, 1981

111) Indian Contract Act, 1872 & Supreme Court's Case Laws" in Nani Palkhiwala Wednesday Law Club

112) Securities and Exchange Board of India Act, 1992 i. e. SEBI Act 1992 & Case Laws on Insiders Trading" in Nani Palkhiwala Wednesday Law Club

113) Moratorium Under Section 14 of IBC, 2016

114) Hindu Marriage Act, 1955

115) Maharashtra Land Revenue Code, 1966

116) 64 Leading Cases of AOR Exam Session 1 :- Cases 1 to16 in Nani Palkhiwala Wednesday Law Club

117) 64 Leading Cases of AOR Exam Session 2: Cases 17 to 32 in Nani Palkhivala Wednesday Law Club

118) 64 Leading Cases of AOR Examination Session 3: Cases 33 to 48 in Nani Palkhivala Wednesday Law Club

119) 64 Leading Cases of AOR Exam Session 4: Cases 49 to 64 in Nani Palkhivala Wednesday Law Club

List Of Adv. Jayprakash Somani's Published Books

1. Supreme Court of India's Leading Case Laws on 'Insolvency & Bankruptcy Code 2016'
2. Bail Matters – Supreme Court's Latest Leading Case Laws
3. Arbitration Matters- Supreme Court's Latest Leading Case Laws
4. Property Matters - Supreme Court's Latest Leading Case Laws
5. Matrimonial Matters- Supreme Court's Latest Leading Case Laws
6. Election Matters- Supreme Court's Latest Leading Case Laws
7. SEBI Matters- Supreme Court's Latest Leading Case Laws
8. Banking Matters- Supreme Court's Latest Leading Case Laws
9. Service Matters- Supreme Court's Latest Leading Case Laws
10. Contempt of Court Matters- Supreme Court's Latest Leading Case Laws
11. Consumer Protection Matters- Supreme Court's Latest Leading Case Laws
12. Corporate Law- Supreme Court's Latest Leading Case Laws
13. Supreme Court's AOR Exam- Leading Cases
14. Armed Force Tribunal - Supreme Court's Latest Leading Case Laws
15. Acquittal From 376 - Supreme Court's Latest Leading Case Laws
16. Negotiable instrument – Supreme Court's Latest Leading Case Laws
17. Contract Act- Supreme Court's Latest Leading Case Laws
18. Insider trading- Supreme Court's Latest Leading Case Laws
19. Foreign Exchange and Management Act- Supreme Court's Latest Leading Case Laws
20. Income Tax Act- Supreme Court's Latest Leading Case Laws
21. Company Law- Supreme Court's Latest Leading Case Laws
22. Competition & Monopoly Matters- Supreme Court's Latest Leading Case Laws
23. Compassionate Appointment- Service Matters- Supreme Court's Latest Leading Case Laws
24. Compulsory Retirement- Service Matters- Supreme Court's Latest Leading Case Laws
25. Voluntary Retirement- Service Matters- Supreme Court's Latest Leading Case Laws

26. Removal/Dismissal/Termination from Service- Supreme Court's Latest Leading Case Laws

27. Seniority- Service Matter- Supreme Court's Latest Leading Case Laws

28. Promotion- Service Matter- Supreme Court's Latest Leading Case Laws

29. Equal Pay for Equal Work- Service Matter- Supreme Court's Latest Leading Case Laws

30. Condition of Service- Service Matter- Supreme Court's Latest Leading Case Laws

31. Customs Act- Supreme Court's Leading Case Laws

32. Information Technology Act- Supreme Court's Leading Case Laws

33. SEC. 125 CR. P. C.- Supreme Court's Leading Case Laws

34. SEC. 498A OF I. P. C.- Supreme Court's Leading Case Laws

35. MOTOR VEHICLE ACT- Supreme Court's Leading Case Laws

36. CONDITION OF SERVICE- SERVICE MATTER- Supreme Court's Leading Case Laws

37. SUSPENSION- SERVICE MATTER- Supreme Court's Leading Case Laws

38. Reservation in SC, ST, OBC- Service Matter- Supreme Court's Leading Case Laws

39. NARCOTIC DRUGS AND PSYCHOTROPIC SUBSTANCES (NDPS) ACT - Supreme Court of India's Latest Leading Case Laws

40. SEC 302 IPC - Supreme Court of India's Latest Leading Case Laws

41. PROTECTION OF CHILDREN FROM SEXUAL OFFENCES ACT (POCSO) - Supreme Court of India's Latest Leading Case Laws

42. PMLA ACT BAIL MATTERS - Supreme Court of India's Leading Case Laws

43. SEC 376 BAIL MATTERS - Supreme Court of India's Leading Case Laws

44. SEC 302 BAIL MATTERS - Supreme Court of India's Leading Case Laws

45. POCSO ACT BAIL MATTERS - Supreme Court of India's Leading Case Laws

46 . JUVENILE JUSTICE ACT- Supreme Court of India's Leading Case Laws

47. TRANSFER OF PROPERTY ACT- Supreme Court of India's Leading Case Laws

48. PROFESSIONAL ETHICS OF ADVOCATES- AOR EXAM-SUPREME COURT'S LEADING CASE LAWS

49. TRANSFER OF PROPERTY ACT- Supreme Court of India's Leading Case Laws

Books are available online in India

1. Notion Press: https://notionpress.com/author/jayprakash_somani

2. Amazon: https://www.amazon.in/s?k=jayprakash+somani

3. Flipkart: https://www.flipkart.com/search?q=Jayprakash%20Somani

Books are available online at International Market

4. Amazon International: https://www.amazon.com/s?k=jayprakash+somani

5. Amazon United Kingdom: https://www.amazon.co.uk/s?k=jayprakash+somani

6. E-Books/Kindle edition at National & International Level: https://www.amazon.in/s?k=jaypraksh+somani

9 798890 660541

Printed by Libri Plureos GmbH in Hamburg,
Germany